Hitler and the Third Reich

Richard Harvey

Historical Consultant:
Dr R. A. H. Robinson,
The University of Birmingham

Stanley Thornes (Publishers) Ltd

First published in 1998 by: Stanley Thornes (Publishers) Ltd,
Delta Place, 27 Bath Road, Cheltenham GL53 7TH,
United Kingdom

01 02 03 04 / 10 9 8 7 6 5 4 3

A catalogue record for this book is available from the British Library.

ISBN 0 7487 3503 8

Illustrated by Hardlines

Printed and bound in Great Britain by Redwood Books, Trowbridge, Wiltshire

Typeset by Tech-Set Ltd, Gateshead, Tyne and Wear

Acknowledgements

With thanks to the following for permission to reproduce photographs in this book:

Imperial War Museum, pages 37, 49
Philip Sauvain Picture Collection, page 19
Weiner Library, page 35

Every effort has been made to contact copyright holders. The publishers apologise to anyone whose rights have been inadvertently overlooked, and will be happy to rectify any errors or omissions.

Contents

How to Use this Book

History at A-level is a more complex and demanding subject than at any preceding level, and it is with these new and higher demands on students in mind that the Pathfinder History series has been written. The basic aim of the book is simple: to enable you to appreciate the important issues that underpin understanding of the principal factors in the nature of Germany after 1918 and the international climate of the time, and how events combined to create an environment exploited by individuals to create and sustain Nazism.

What this book does not do is provide a single source of all the answers needed for exam success. The very nature of A-level study demands that you use a range of resources in your studies, in order to build up the understanding of different interpretations on issues, and develop your own argument on exam topics. Pathfinder can help make this subject more accessible by defining the key issues, giving an initial understanding of them and helping students to define questions for further investigation. It concentrates on the fundamentals of Nazism and its history; the important issues, events and characters of the period that you must understand, and which the examiners will want to see that you know.

Hence it becomes more of a guide book to the subject, and can be used whenever you want within the A-level course; as an introduction, as a reminder revision text or throughout the course each time a new topic is started. Pathfinder also has several important features to help you get to grips with Hitler and Nazism.

FEATURES OF PATHFINDER

The book follows the three basic stages of the A-level process, explaining why they are important and why you are doing them. The three sections of the book are thus Overview, Enquiry and Investigation, and Review. These describe the main methods for studying History at A-level; so, for example, when you answer a question on the political background of the 1933 elections, you will recall why this book approaches this topic with these three headings in mind.

Key Issues and Key Skills

Pathfinder is written around three basic principles. The first is that it covers the most important events, themes, ideas and concepts of the subject, called the *Key Issues*. The second is that there are levels or tiers to these issues, so that a major question is broken down into its contributory questions and issues and is thus easier to understand. And the third principle is that there are fundamental skills that you must develop and employ as historians at this level, and these are referred to as the *Key Skills*.

These principles combine in Section 1, where **The Big Picture** sets the whole scene of the topic, and identifies the most important periods and events within the topic. What **The Key Issues** does is to establish what the author believes are the fundamental questions and answers to the subject as a whole, and then discuss these in more detail by raising all the contributory questions contained within the main question. Each period is discussed in more detail in Section 2, and you will see page references for each appropriate chapter. Each period thus also has its own issues and concepts, to provide a second tier of Key Issues. Finally, the **What to Read, how to Read, where to Find it and how to Use it** section offers hints and advice on the active study skills you will be using in A-level history. The main focus of the book is Section 2, called **Enquiry and Investigation** because this is exactly what you are being asked to do for most of the time during the A-level process. You are making historical enquiries and learning how to interpret sources and information every time you look at a document, analyse a photograph or read around a topic. Each chapter takes as its title one of the periods identified in The Big Picture, and each one also identifies what you need to bear in mind when working on that particular issue or theme. There is a useful little tab at the start of each double-page spread that summarises the most important aspects of the topic and identifies the skills that you will use in studying it.

These are Key Skills, although you could think of them as key study skills if you prefer. There are a number of them, and they can be grouped under the following headings and with these helpful definitions:

Skills for collecting information from historical sources

Analysis: breaking down information into component parts (making notes under section headings, for example).

Interpretation: considering the implications of information and cross-referencing to other sources or contextual knowledge to develop your understanding further. (Skills used within this are actually inference, deduction, extrapolation, interpolation, recall and synthesis.)

Evaluation: assessing the validity of sources and hence the implications for the reliability of its information.

Recording: arranging information into sections that allow easy retrieval as required. For example making linear notes (good for large amounts of information), diagrams and flowcharts or mind maps (good for establishing relationships between sections of information).

Skills for applying and using information

Explanation: using information to show how and why something happened.

Assessment: weighing up possible explanations or interpretations.

Forming hypotheses: setting up an explanation or judgement for further testing.

Testing hypotheses: using information to support and challenge a hypothesis to improve it.

Setting a thesis: using the information to present, support and sustain a tested hypothesis and an explanation of historical processes.

You will see that some are flagged more often than others, and there may be others, such as chronology, that are not defined here. However, the important point to remember is that these are the skills that the A-level historian has to have available for use, and that you are actually using them all the time already. The aim is to reinforce these skills for you, and to enable you to see how you are using them and why.

Section 3 Review then brings all the interpretations, investigations and issues that you have looked at on Hitler and the Third Reich into

one place. Synthesis is the bringing together of issues, arguments and judgements into overall answers. It also poses answers to what the author considers to be the main issues identified in Section 1. **Questions and Answers** then takes the information, knowledge and hypotheses and applies them to more detailed essay answers, of the style that you might find or that you might write in an exam. The **Final Review** is something of the author's own thoughts and conclusions to the subject on a broad level.

MARGINS AND ICONS

Pathfinder divides material as part of the main aim of focusing attention on the most important issues. Hence the main central narrative discusses and interprets information and, although detailed, cannot provide all of the information on its topic. It can be integrated and supplemented with more detailed works, articles and documents.

All other sorts of information appear in the margins and you will see the following icons used alongside them. Not all icons appear in every chapter and some chapters have other features included as well, but the icons should help you to manage the extra information given on topics:

 Documents, historiography and sources – quotes from texts, individuals and passages

 Suggested headings for notes

 Suggested further reading

 Sample activities and exam-style questions

 General hints, study tips and advice

 Key words

This book is a history of Germany between 1918 and 1945. In those years, Germany had two very different systems of government: the Weimar Republic and the Third Reich. One was liberal and democratic, and the other a totalitarian dictatorship, but both had an enormous effect on the German people and on Europe.

The next four pages provide a brief account of what happened in those years. Read them and they will give you an overview or, as the title says, the Big Picture.

This is just an introduction to the book and the period. It aims to set what you will cover in the subject in context. By looking at everything briefly you should gain an idea of where and how all the pieces fit together.

If you are not sure what some words mean, have a look for the Key words icon in the margin, as here:

The Big Picture: Germany 1918–1945

THE WEIMAR REPUBLIC 1918–1924 (see pages 14–17)

- The loss of the Great War and the hardships suffered by the German people lead to a revolution in Germany and the proclamation of a Republic.
- Because of unrest in Berlin, the new regime has to meet at Weimar. It signs the unpopular Treaty of Versailles; and adopts a new constitution which, while fair to all, leads to a succession of weak governments.
- The Republic faces a number of armed uprisings, and hostility from political parties of both the extreme right and left.
- A huge national debt, the French occupation of the Ruhr and hyperinflation lead to near economic collapse.
- By taking difficult decisions, and with the help of American loans, the new government of Stresemann stabilises Germany, and sees it towards a period of apparent growth and prosperity.

HITLER AND THE NAZI PARTY 1919–1929 (see pages 18–21)

- Adolf Hitler emerges from poverty and obscurity to join, and later lead, the NSDAP or Nazi Party, a small but extreme right-wing nationalist, socialist and anti-Jewish party.
- Hitler leads a revolt against the government, in Munich, but it is crushed, and he is imprisoned. While in prison he writes *Mein Kampf*, his concept of a future Germany: racist, expansionist, and with himself as supreme leader.
- The Weimar Republic appears to flourish from 1924 to 1929, but the prosperity (in which many people do not share) is based on American loans, and political instability remains.
- Hitler reforms the Nazi Party on his release from prison, but it remains a minor political force, picking up protest votes, until the Great Depression sweeps in from America.

THE END OF WEIMAR GERMANY 1929–1933 (see pages 22–25)

- As the Great Depression strikes, American loans are withdrawn, industries contract, banks close and unemployment rises towards 6 million. Politicians seem unable to solve the crisis, and elections are called.
- The Nazis have developed sophisticated propaganda techniques, and by promising all things to all people win a massive increase in the vote in 1930, and become a mainstream political force.

- Governments now only remain in office by presidential decree and rule ineffectually. In the July 1932 election, the Nazis double their vote and become the largest party.
- The last days of the Weimar Republic are played out to backstairs intrigue. Cabinets come and go until the President, Hindenburg, appoints Hitler as Chancellor of a coalition government.

THE NAZI STATE 1933–1945 (SEE PAGES 26–29)

- Using presidential decrees and the power of the state, Hitler calls and fights another election, but the Nazis still gain under half the vote.
- By a mixture of naked force and pressure, Hitler gets an Enabling Act, giving his government full powers. The Nazis now seize state governments, ban trades unions and other political parties, and Nazify Germany.
- Hitler eliminates the SA, and on Hindenburg's death becomes *Führer*. The Nazi Party attaches itself to state organisations; and the Nazis persecute the churches and undermine the army.
- Nazi Germany becomes a country of competing empires, each headed by its own dictator, controlling culture, youth, the economy and so on. At the head of the nation stands Hitler, the sole arbiter, and source of supreme power.

totalitarian – a regime that suppresses all rights and freedoms, and demands that all people support it

republic – a form of government characterised by a President, as opposed to a King or Emperor

constitution – the principles and rules of government

hyperinflation – extreme loss of monetary value

nationalist – a supporter of country and culture

socialist – an advocate of the sharing of wealth and power by the people

propaganda – false or distorted information intended to persuade people to agree with a point of view

presidential decree – a law signed by the President and not needing the approval of Parliament

Führer – leader of the German people and state

dictator – a ruler with absolute power and authority

This map shows how the size and shape of the country changed between the two world wars

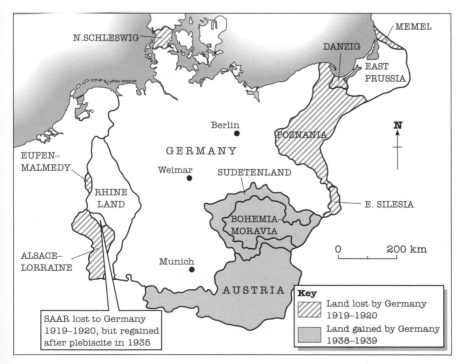

SAAR lost to Germany 1919–1920, but regained after plebiscite in 1935

Key

Land lost by Germany 1919–1920

Land gained by Germany 1938–1939

Remember as you look at The Big Picture that this is an introduction to the book and the period. It aims to set what you are going to learn about in context, and to enable you to gain some basic idea, quite quickly, of how events and issues are related to one another.

As you look through this summary of the period, you will see that it covers many aspects of German history in the Weimar and Nazi eras. Because of the nature of the changes that take place at this time, most of the history here will concentrate on the politics of the era; but foreign affairs and war also take up a large part of this book. On the other hand, economics and social issues also loom large, while at the same time giving a flavour of what it was like to live in Germany at this time.

Although you may well have studied this at GCSE level, you probably won't have studied the Weimar Republic in any depth. Even if you have, you should find much here that is fresh to you, and presented in much greater depth than you have been used to. Remember: this is A-level. It will require you to know the detail of the period in a way that you did not have to for GCSE.

If you work your way through this book, you will find that you know a great deal more about this period than you ever did before – and, more to the point, you will understand more. Some of the issues that you will cover here are central to the history of Europe over the past 70 years; some of them shaped European history for 40 years; and some of them are still with us to this day.

LIFE IN NAZI GERMANY 1933–1939 (see pages 30–33)

- The Nazis 'solve' the unemployment problem by public works that regenerate trade, investing in industry, rearmament and conscription. Industrial workers gain improved working conditions and leisure opportunities, but lose union rights.
- The middle classes and the peasants benefit from Nazi reform.
- Young people are indoctrinated at school, and are forced to join Nazi youth movements outside school.
- Women are discouraged from working in favour of being wives and mothers, but such policies are not very effective.
- Propaganda and censorship are used to influence what Germans do and say, and even how they think.
- The Nazis use 'law-and-order' methods to suppress crime, but also to persecute those groups it considers to be 'outsiders'.

THE NAZIS AND THE JEWS 1933–1945 (see pages 34–37)

- The Nazis aim to rid Germany of the Jewish 'cancer', and are aided in this by latent anti-Semitism. A series of increasingly restrictive laws, and popular actions, put pressure on the Jewish community to emigrate, and many do.
- *Kristallnacht* launches a full-scale pogrom, with Jewish property destroyed and thousands of Jews imprisoned. The persecution is intensified, and by 1939 those Jews left in Germany have become an unwanted and hated minority.
- The war in Europe brings a further 3 million Jews into Nazi hands, and deportations start to the ghettos. The invasion of the Soviet Union leads to the wholesale mass murder of Russian and Ukrainian Jews by the SS.
- The ordering of the 'Final Solution' brings about the mass extermination of the European Jewish community, as some 5 million Jews are killed in the genocide of the death camps.

THE GERMAN OPPOSITION TO THE NAZIS 1933–1945 (see pages 38–41)

- Many individuals work silently against the Nazi regime.
- Workers, intellectuals, the churches and young people form underground groups to protest, but organised opposition is difficult in a police state, and most groups are crushed.
- To counter the possibility of a popular revolt, the Nazis try to ensure that civilian morale always remains high.
- The army, and the rest of the establishment, come to see that Hitler is leading Germany to disaster, and make plots to destroy him, but none are successful. The opposition fails.

GERMAN FOREIGN POLICY 1933–1939 (see pages 42–45)

- Hitler determines to fulfill his concept of Germany's destiny, of all German *Volk* in one *Reich* (including *Lebensraum* if necessary), and works to destroy the Versailles settlement, isolate France and ally with Britain or Italy.

- British and French reluctance to work together or contain Hitler bring him foreign policy successes; and Nazi affinity with Italian fascism culminates in the Rome–Berlin axis.

- The *Anschluss* with Austria and the destruction of Czechoslovakia greatly enlarge German power in central Europe, and force Britain and France to guarantee Poland's security.

- Hitler signs alliances with Italy and Russia as a way of gaining Poland, not believing that Britain and France will fight over it. When they do, he finds himself with a major war in Europe which he does not want.

THE THIRD REICH AT WAR 1939–1945 (see pages 46–49)

- Using *Blitzkrieg* techniques, the Germans overrun Poland, and western and southeastern Europe, and wage war in North Africa and the North Atlantic, but are unable to conquer Britain. The invasion of the Soviet Union is the culmination of all Hitler's policies, but it is a war he cannot win. When he declares war on the USA, he is doomed.

- The German economy, while geared up for war, operates on an almost peacetime footing until 1942. Only then does it adopt the practices necessary for total war.

- The powers of the Nazi Party and the SS expand during the war, tightening their grip over every aspect of life.

- Civilian morale remains high until the Russian campaign, but as victories give way to defeats, and the effects of the allied bombing hit home, the consequences of war become apparent.

- The last year of the war brings catastrophe to Germany, and when Hitler commits suicide, he leaves behind a shattered, occupied and divided country.

The Nazis and History

The Nazi period of German history lasted for only 12 years and 3 months, yet within that time-span were packed some of the most cataclysmic events ever to overtake Germany or Europe. These events were caused, in large part, by the Nazis and their leader, Adolf Hitler, which is why they are so important in the study of History.

There are other reasons why the Third Reich is a major period for study. One is that it is all of a piece: nothing like it was seen in history before 1933 and, fortunately, nothing like it has been seen since 1945. It is true that it shared similarities with aspects of other European fascist movements of the 1920s and 1930s, but in its totality it stands apart.

Another reason why it is studied in such depth is that in 1945 almost all of its records and archives fell into the hands of the Allies. The materials released – documents, signals, letters and so on – meant that historians could study the regime straightaway, without waiting for years for such archives to be released (many, of course, never are).

It would be wrong to study Nazi Germany for these reasons alone. The period may be fascinating, but it should be a fascination tinged with outrage and horror. The destruction, suffering and slaughter caused by the Nazis is amongst the worst by any regime in history. To study it should act as a warning – to ensure that such a regime, with all its terrible consequences, never happens again.

What are 'Key Issues'?

'Key Issues' are a way of studying History with a purpose. They are the why and sometimes the how of History rather than just the what.

As you know, the study of A-level History is much more than learning about 'what happened'. At GCSE level you should have learnt that, in addition to describing facts and chronology, you had to use evidence and explain different interpretations of events. Elsewhere in this book you will find that you need to investigate, analyse and explain historical events in order to achieve success at A-level.

The 'Key Issues' are the questions that you should ask yourself when studying History. It is all too easy sometimes to read about history but not really understand it. Textbooks too often tell you things without showing you their importance, or why they happened in the first place, and leave you wondering about why such-and-such is in the text. This can be very frustrating, and often leaves you with an incomplete understanding of the subject.

A real understanding of history comes from being able to ask questions as well as give answers, and this is what the 'Key Issues' are designed for. As you work your way through the text, you will find that there are 'Key Issues' on every spread. These are designed to help you ask the questions that are important for each topic. By asking them, and keeping them in mind as you work through the chapters, you should reach a much deeper understanding of the topics than you otherwise might.

The Key Issues

1. WHY DID THE WEIMAR REPUBLIC FAIL?

It was the failure of the Weimar Republic that opened the door for Hitler and the Nazi Party in Germany. It is crucial then to establish why the Weimar system collapsed within 14 years, and how this could have come about.

The first thing to consider is why the Weimar Republic came into existence in the first place. Why did the violent and chaotic circumstances of its birth haunt it; why did its Constitution lead to weak, rather than strong and popular government; and why was it always associated with the Treaty of Versailles? The Republic was dogged throughout its life by problems. How did both the political and economic problems that the Republic faced affect its future; and although it appeared to stabilise in its middle years, were these years as stable and prosperous as they seemed to be?

The Great Depression hit Weimar Germany very hard. Why was this, and why did the politicians seem to have no answers to it? Why did the politicians seem to be unable to convince a sceptical electorate that they could find solutions to the country's problems; and why did they allow the country to be ruled by presidential decree, destroying the credibility of the Weimar system? Finally, was the Weimar Republic inherently weak, and doomed to failure, or was it little different from other European states of this time?

2. WHY DID HITLER AND THE NAZIS, AND NOT SOME OTHER POLITICAL FORCE, COME TO POWER IN 1933?

Everyone knows the importance of Hitler and the Nazi Party to German and European history; but why should this have been so? Who was Hitler, and how did his early life shape his ideas? Why and how should the ideas and experiences of Hitler have shaped the form and philosophy of the Nazi Party? Was the Nazi Party always an important political force; and how near to oblivion was Hitler in 1928, when he was still the little-known leader of a minor political party?

Why did the Great Depression both save and make Hitler? What factors led the fortunes of the Nazi Party to rise so dramatically after the 1930 election? What appeal did the Nazis have that attracted so many people to vote for them, rather than for other right-wing parties? Why did the parties of the centre and the left, who retained their support in the country, fail to work together, or fail to convince the President and his advisers that they could govern? Why could the conservative elites find no one else to form a government, and why did they believe that they could tame Hitler, and so hand him the government of Germany on a plate?

3. DID THE NAZIS ACHIEVE A 'SOCIAL REVOLUTION' IN GERMANY?

The Nazi dream was of one people in one state under one leader, marching forwards together. How were the Nazis able to lay the foundations for this ideal by establishing a dictatorship in Germany so quickly; how did they organise the state to achieve these aims; how did they change the way of life of the German people; and to what extent did they turn the German economy around and gain popular support for their programme?

Why did the dream not become reality? How much of an active underground opposition existed all through the Nazi era; why did young people rebel against conformity; how many women remained in work; why did artists emigrate; and why did propaganda have only a limited effect? Did the increasing interference of the Nazi Party and the SS in German life show the bankruptcy of Nazi ideology? Did war destroy the 'social revolution', or had it already begun to decay?

4. WHY WAS THERE A GENOCIDE IN EUROPE BETWEEN 1939 AND 1945?

Why did racial theories, especially anti-Semitism, lie at the base of Nazi ideology? Did Hitler believe in a pure Aryan *Volk*, and why were homosexuals, gypsies, those with mental or physical handicaps and particularly Jews considered to be a 'cancer' that had to be cut out? Why was no effort spared to isolate or expel the carriers of this 'cancer' in the early years of the Reich?

Why did the war in Europe end the possibility of expulsion, and bring millions more Jews under Nazi control? Why did extermination become the preferred option? Could it be hidden or camouflaged by the actions of war? Why was a deliberate policy of mass murder applied to the groups of 'outsiders', and why were enough Germans prepared to co-operate with this for long enough to enable the policy to be followed through?

5. WHY WAS GERMANY AT WAR FROM 1939 TO 1945?

Why did Hitler aim to destroy the Versailles settlement, and did he intentionally want to re-establish Germany as a great power in Europe, and expand the German Reich into Poland and the Soviet Union? What did he need in order to do this; and why did British, French and Italian reluctance to contain him mean that he achieved his initial aims without fighting until 1939? What miscalculation drove him into war over Poland, and why should the need to secure Europe before turning east have kept Germany at war until 1941?

Why did Hitler's invasion of the Soviet Union, and his declaration of war on the USA, mean a war of attrition to the finish? To what extent was the German economy on a war footing from 1942, and to what extent did the war affect every aspect of life of the German people? What consequences did the war bring to the German people, and to the state of Germany itself, after 1945?

How can Key Issues help?

As you're probably not used to asking yourself questions as you read through a history book, there are questions designed as 'Key Issues' on every spread to help you. As you look through the book, you should see that the type of 'Key Issue' question gradually changes. To begin with, when you are not used to them, they are very specific, for example:

'Was the Treaty of Versailles important to the (Weimar) Republic?'

or

'Why did the Great Depression hit Weimar Germany so hard?'

However, as you progress further into the book the 'Key Issues' become more general, providing you with only an outline, and allowing you to think of your own questions. For example:

'Why did the Holocaust happen in Europe between 1939 and 1945?'

or

'To what extent did the Second World War affect the German people?'

The aim is, by the end of each topic and the book, for you to be thinking of your own 'Key Issues'.

Books and information

Historical information used to mean only one thing: the written word. Books, monographs, magazine articles and, as primary evidence, documents, diaries and letters: these were what the historian used to write History; and History was, almost exclusively, a written medium.

Today, most history books use not only text but diagrams, drawings and photographs to illustrate their content. Moreover, history books are now seen as only a part of what History is about. In this century, because of technological change, other means of recording history have become available.

Through film, we can now see the Nazis marching through Germany; through sound, we can hear Hitler making speeches; on television, former SS officers can explain their beliefs and actions; and on CD-ROM, sound, pictures, film and diagrams can be brought together in a multimedia format.

The written word is still important: but today films or television series such as *The Nazis* are just as important, and as valid, as sources of information about the Third Reich. These don't replace the written word, but they do complement it, and they often offer views of history that books cannot. Seeing film of Auschwitz or Belsen places you immediately in that situation, and engages more of your senses than any book ever could.

History is no longer just about reading books: use any piece of information you come across to 'round out' your view of the past.

What to Read, how to Read, where to Find it and how to Use it

1. WHERE TO FIND INFORMATION

The first place to find information about the Weimar and Nazi era in German history is in this book. However, that should not be the last place. This book aims to help you find a path through the complex and often difficult history of these times, but at 64 pages long it cannot hope to be comprehensive. To learn more, you will need to use a library. A good library should have audio and visual material, as well as the printed page; and if it doesn't have what you want, it should be able to get it for you. Just ask at the counter.

Most libraries divide their space into sections devoted to different subjects, so you should find one area for History. You will need 20th-century German History, from 1918 to 1945. If the library has a Dewey numbering system, look under 943.085 for books on the Weimar Republic, and under 943.086 for information about Nazi Germany. As well as the general section, most libraries have a Reference section: you may well find good information on 20th-century European History here, but you won't be able to borrow the books.

2. ACTIVE INFORMATION-SEEKING

When you have found a book (or film or video) that you want, what do you do with it? If you just read it (or watch it), you won't learn very much. The key to success is to read or watch *selectively*, concentrating on those parts that you need. For example, if you want to find out about Hitler's early life, look at the **chapter headings** at the front of the book and read just those chapters concerned with his formative years. If you want to study the *Gestapo*, look in the **Index** at the back of the book and find the pages on which it is mentioned. In this way you will only read the parts of books that you need.

One book, however, may have a very individual view of its subject, so it is very important that, when reading at A-level, you read around the subject; that is, you read a number of books or articles on the same subject to get a balanced view. In this way you should be able to learn all you need to know about a subject, and form a view in your own mind as to which interpretation of the subject is likely to be correct. To find other books look in a **Bibliography**: a list of other books that an author has consulted, usually near the back of that book. In *this* book I have suggested other books to read, but throughout the text, rather than at the back.

The main point about active reading is that you can only do it best when you have an overall understanding of the period; for example, as provided by this book.

3. NOTE-TAKING

Most people find that when they read a book they absorb a certain amount of information: but when they make notes on what they are reading they take in a great deal more. Taking and making notes on what you are studying is good for learning.

Simply rewriting what you have just read is, however, a waste of time. What you need to do is to summarise the information that you find *in a form that is useful to you*. As I write elsewhere in this book, don't just copy things down without thinking. Try to have an objective in mind when making notes; think about the questions you want to find answers for, and use the notes as information to answer those questions. I have suggested lots of Headings for Notes in this book: they are designed to help you write down the notes that you need in order to answer the questions that you have.

There are also different ways of making notes. Many people find that the traditional way of note-taking, of writing lines of text on a page, is unsatisfactory by itself: it keeps information in blocks, with no way of connecting it together. An alternative is the information diagram: put the core concept – for example, Hitler's Early Life – in a box in the centre of your page, and radiate lines out from it like the branches of a tree. For example, 'Family' might lead to 'Parents' and 'Siblings'; 'Parents' could branch to 'Father' and 'Mother'; and 'Father' to 'Age', 'Job', 'Character' and so on. Use the system that suits you best. Although these may be two different approaches that serve different purposes, they also complement each other and combine to improve learning and understanding.

4. PERSONAL ORGANISATION

Most of you reading this will be studying A-level History as only a part of what you are doing: you will have other things competing for your time and attention, and you will wonder how you will be able to fit it all in. The key is organisation – planning your time effectively so that you can use it well.

Most people find the study of History challenging as well as enjoyable. It is easy to get swept up with enthusiasm at first and spend a whole day reading and making notes on a book: the trouble is that you then feel exhausted and only come back to it much later when deadlines for essays and so on loom, and then your work is rushed. This 'stop–go' way of working benefits no one. It is much better to sit down and make realistic assessments of how much time you can, or are likely to, spend on History, and work out a timetable.

Don't expect to spend more than a couple of hours a session on History: you will feel very jaded if you do – better a few sessions spread over a week than a whole day devoted to it. Try to strike a balance between reading, watching, note-taking and answering questions. Above all, try to stick with any timetable that you make: time lost will seldom be caught up, and if you do a little and often you will minimise any time that you do lose.

Technology

Although History is a subject that deals with the past, don't feel that you have to be bound to the past to study it. Handwritten notes may be the traditional way to collect information, but that is only because, in times past, writing notes by hand from a teacher's lecture was the only way for the student to acquire those notes for him- or herself.

Today there are alternatives. For example, a teacher could photocopy notes for guidance, and then use the teaching time to explain the concepts that are in them. Recording a lecture on audio or video gives the student the opportunity to play back the tape and go over again anything that he or she is not sure of.

A student no longer even needs to rely on the teacher or on information being within physical reach. As you have seen, libraries can order books from anywhere in the country; television is no longer restricted to a few terrestrial channels but can now be accessed on cable or via satellite; and the Internet has opened up the libraries of the world to anyone who wants to browse through them.

There should now be no excuse for not finding all the information you need to study History. If anything, you may find that you suffer from problems of information overload: which is why it is vital that you read this chapter as carefully as any other to find the best way of studying the history of Germany from 1918 to 1945.

Kaiser – the German emperor, Wilhelm II (who reigned from 1890 to 1918)

soviets – revolutionary councils

Spartakists – revolutionary socialists, who wanted to overthrow the institutions of prewar, Imperial Germany, and establish a people's dictatorship

Freikorps — armed, nationalist ex-soldiers, anti-socialist but also anti-democratic

Diktat – a dictated peace, which Germany had no say in

Länd – a German province (plural *Länder*)

Reichstag – the federal German Parliament

The Foundation of the Weimar Republic: 1918–1919

GERMANY AND THE GREAT WAR

By November 1918, it was apparent to many in Germany that the war was lost. In four years of fighting, over 2 million German troops had been killed, and millions more had been left with physical or mental scars. A series of severe winters and poor harvests had led to a fuel crisis and food rationing, and now thousands of civilians were dying from cold and hunger. The British blockade and the demands of the war had caused enormous economic dislocation, leading to the disruption of industries, to shortages and to inflation. In late September, the German generals Hindenburg and Ludendorff had advised the *Kaiser* that the war was lost; in October, a new government had instituted reforms that would make Germany a parliamentary democracy with a constitutional monarchy, and had opened armistice negotiations with the Allies; but all this proved to be too little, too late.

THE GERMAN REVOLUTION

In early November 1918, the sailors of the German High Seas Fleet at Kiel refused to obey orders. News of this mutiny spread through the country, and by 8 November workers' and soldiers' councils, based on the Russian *soviets*, had been set up in many towns and cities. On the next day there was a general strike in Berlin, and the *Kaiser*, faced with a disintegrating country, fled to Holland. Ebert, the leader of the working class and trade union based German Social Democratic Party (SPD) formed a government and, fearing a Soviet-style revolution, proclaimed a Republic. To maintain law and order and ensure stability, the government negotiated agreements with, and gained the support of, the army, employers and trades unions; and on 11 November an armistice was signed.

BIRTH OF THE WEIMAR REPUBLIC

The new Republic had a difficult birth. In January 1919 the *Spartakists*, an extreme left-wing group, attempted an armed uprising which the government had to put down using both regular troops and the *Freikorps*, groups of right-wing ex-soldiers. Elections to a new National Assembly were held, with the SPD, the DDP (Liberals) and the ZP (Catholic Centre Party) gaining most of the votes; but a series of strikes and riots in Berlin forced the Assembly to move to the town of Weimar to meet. A short-lived Soviet Republic was proclaimed in Bavaria in April, but it was put down using federal German forces.

THE TREATY OF VERSAILLES

In this state of chaos, the Republic had to deal with two key issues: the formal ending of the war, and its own constitution. Germans believed that the treaty to end the war was going to be based on Wilson's 14 Points, so when the draft peace treaty was published in May 1919 it was universally condemned. The loss of large parts of Germany, and of all of her colonies; the disarmament clauses; the 'war guilt' clause and the large reparations demanded; and the exclusion of Germany from the League of Nations – all of these things were seen by most Germans as a shameful *Diktat*, an unfair and unreasonable attack upon the German nation and state. By signing the Treaty of Versailles the Republic, however unfairly, was forever associated with it; and that signature came to be used, in the future, by nationalist and anti-republican movements as a propaganda weapon with which to attack the Weimar system.

THE WEIMAR CONSTITUTION

The adoption of the Weimar constitution in July 1919 made Germany a federal republic: each of the *Länder*, or states, had its own government with powers over such things as the police and education, while the federal government kept control of foreign affairs, the armed forces and taxation. There was universal suffrage, and proportional representation, but while this ensured that all points of view could be heard in the *Reichstag*, it encouraged many small political parties, which led to weak coalition governments – 15 over the 14-year period of the Republic. A wide range of civil liberties were guaranteed, but the police, the judiciary, the civil service and the education system remained in their old form – conservative and reactionary – and most of their members were unenthusiastic about the Republic. Lastly, by having an elected President, and giving him considerable powers – including appointing the chancellor and government and, in an emergency, being able to rule by presidential decree – the possibility was created of a future, but still perfectly legal, non-parliamentary government.

> You need to know what effect Losing the War had on Germany; what The German Revolution was; what happened in The *Spartakist* Revolt; how the Terms of the Versailles Treaty upset the Germans; and whether the Weimar constitution gave Strong or Weak Government.

Read more about the subject. There are many books on the Weimar Republic, but for now you need only look at the sections in these books that cover its foundation, the Treaty of Versailles and the Weimar constitution. You could try books on *The Weimar Republic* by E. Kolb (Unwin Hyman, 1988) or J. W. Hiden (Longman, 1996); or, for a general introduction, W. Carr, *A History of Germany 1815–1990* (Edward Arnold, 1991).

About the Key Skills

As well as acquiring knowledge and understanding of the subject, A-level History is about developing the skills that a historian needs. At GCSE level you should have learnt to describe and narrate, to order chronologically, to identify and evaluate sources, and to explain different interpretations of events.

At A-level you must go a stage further. You should be able to **investigate** a series of events by yourself through looking at a wide range of information; **analyse** what you have discovered by way of discussing, comparing and judging; **interpret** and **explain** events by considering a wide range of evidence; **empathise** by understanding historical period and attitudes; and, above all, **assess** the importance or significance of various factors.

This may sound difficult, but remember that it isn't a case of doing it all at once. Each chapter of this book will have its own Key Skills to assist you in identifying what part of the process requires what skill.

THE KEY ISSUES

- How much political opposition was there to the Weimar Republic?
- How did the economic problems of the Republic affect German people in the short and long term?

THE KEY SKILLS

Investigation

Analysis

WHAT YOU HAVE TO DO

Use these skills, your reading and the notes you have made to answer some of the Key Issues in this chapter.

What was the extent of Political Opposition/Support for Weimar; how did Reparations affect German debt; what happened in The Ruhr Crisis; what were the effects of Hyperinflation; and how was Germany Stabilised?

Putsch – an armed uprising

Reichsmark – the German currency, much devalued since the war

Passive resistance – non-violent opposition to French troops by Germans refusing to work

Rentenmark – the new currency, backed by the value of all the land in Germany

The Crisis of the Weimar Republic: 1920–1924

ARMED UPRISINGS

Outright opposition to the Republic continued throughout its early years. The *Freikorps* units, who had prevented the communist takeover in 1919, hated it as much as anyone, and were responsible for the Kapp *Putsch* of March 1920, when they marched on Berlin and tried to set up a new regime. Although the army did nothing to stop them, a general strike called by the government quickly paralysed the country, and after four days the *Putsch* collapsed. Other revolts included communist uprisings in Saxony in 1921 and in Hamburg in 1923, which were crushed by the police and army.

POLITICAL PROBLEMS

Many political groups were also hostile to the Republic. The far right rejected Weimar and all it stood for. Conservatives and nationalists could not forget that the 'November Criminals' (by which they meant socialists, republicans, Jews, democrats and so on) had, in their eyes, betrayed the country by signing the armistice when the war had not been lost, thus 'stabbing Germany in the back', accepting Versailles and overthrowing the monarchy. On the extreme left, the Communists and some socialists (the heirs of the *Spartakists*) wanted a continuing revolution, a one-party state and a fundamental shift to the left in the fabric of German life. They frightened many people with their talk of revolution and were, like the far right, opposed to the whole Weimar system.

The Republic, then, had a fundamental problem. Throughout its life, neither far left nor far right were prepared to co-operate with the centrist parties that governed it. They did not want to change governments, but to destroy the whole system. This meant that all Weimar governments had to be shifting coalitions of the centre-left or centre-right, which added to its instability. Moreover, when people shifted their votes in large numbers to the left and right in the 1930s, the centrist parties were unable to gather enough support to form majority governments.

ECONOMIC PROBLEMS

As well as political problems, the Republic faced economic ones. It had been left with a huge national debt from the war, and a *Reichsmark* that was fast losing its value. Unwilling to increase taxation or cut expenditure to balance the books, it continued to borrow heavily. The bill for reparations, presented to the Republic in 1921, of £6600 million, simply added to the debt, and the government resorted to printing money in order to pay it. This disastrous policy destabilised the currency even further and the value of the mark collapsed.

In the middle of this runaway inflation, French and Belgian troops occupied the Ruhr. Unable to pay its reparations instalments, Germany had defaulted, so the French moved in to collect payments in kind. *Passive resistance* by the workers prevented this, but also stopped the flow of goods and taxes within Germany, leaving the government with no choice but to print more money to pay the wages and pensions of its workers, and to buy the coal and other goods that it desperately needed.

The government now lost control of the financial situation, and hyperinflation set in, as money became worthless and people reverted to a barter economy. People with debts, either mortgages or loans, were able to pay them off quickly with this worthless money and benefited; as did farmers, whose income rose with high food prices, and businessmen with goods to sell. On the other hand, anyone with savings, pensions or annuities, which usually meant the old or the middle class, lost their money and faced ruin. More importantly, they also lost their faith in the Weimar Republic.

STABILISATION OF THE REPUBLIC

The appointment of Stresemann as Chancellor in August 1923 was a turning point. By taking difficult decisions – ending passive resistance, cutting government expenditure and introducing a new currency, the *Rentenmark* – inflation was halted and the currency stabilised. Moreover, a new look was taken at the problem of reparations, and the Dawes Plan of 1924 geared payments for five years directly to Germany's capacity to pay, and provided for large international loans to the country to help cover this.

In a matter of months, the position of the Weimar Republic appeared to have been transformed: it had come through its crises, and seemed set to enjoy a period of stability, growth and prosperity. Dark forces, however, continued to lurk just below the surface: in November of 1923 another *Putsch* had been attempted in Munich. Among its leaders was an extreme nationalist few people outside Germany had ever heard of: Adolf Hitler.

Political parties in the Weimar Republic

Left   KPD – Communist Party. Opposed Weimar. Worked for a revolutionary overthrow of society.
USPD – Independent Socialists. Opposed Weimar. Wanted radical political and social change.

Centre-left   SPD – Social Democratic Party. Supported Weimar. Party of the working class and trades unions.
DDP – Democratic Party. Supported Weimar. A liberal party supported by the middle classes.

Centre   ZP – Centre Party. Supported Weimar. Attracted support from Catholics across the social spectrum.

Centre-right   BVP – Bavarian People's Party. Supported Weimar. Strong support from Catholics in Bavaria.
DVP – People's Party. Supported Weimar. The party of Gustav Stresemann and his supporters.

Right   DNVP – National People's Party. Opposed Weimar. Conservative, monarchist, pro big business.
NSDAP – National Socialist (Nazi). Opposed Weimar. Strongly nationalist and anti-Semitic.

When reading further about these topics, try these texts: G. Layton, *From Bismarck to Hitler: Germany 1890–1933* (Hodder & Stoughton, 1995) and J. Wright, 'Stresemann and Weimar', *History Today*, Oct. 1989.

Evidence

For A-level, sources of evidence are likely to be more complex than you are used to, but will still be as historically relevant. You simply have to investigate them more thoroughly, and recognise that they can only tell you a part of the story – if sometimes a very important part. For example, the effects of hyperinflation ...

'The expense of even the most essential foodstuffs – I need only indicate fats, meat and bread – and the want of coal, linen, clothing and soap, prevent any improvement in living conditions. The height to which prices have climbed may be shown by the fact that as of February 15th [1923] wholesale prices have risen on the average to 5967 times the peacetime level, those of foodstuffs to 4902 times ... For many people meat has become altogether a rarity ... health levels are deteriorating ever more seriously ... There are increases in stomach disorders and food poisoning, which are the result of eating spoiled foods ... Just recently a well known German professor has died of hunger.'
From a speech by the head of the Reich Department of Health, February 1923

THE KEY ISSUES

- How the early life of Adolf Hitler shaped his ideas.
- How the ideas and experiences of Hitler shaped the form and philosophy of the Nazi Party.
- The importance of the ideas of nationalism and socialism, and how a political movement could demonstrate both.

THE KEY SKILLS

Investigation
Analysis
Assessment

WHAT YOU HAVE TO DO

No A-level question will ask you about Hitler and the Nazi Party in isolation; but you need to find out where National Socialism stood in relation to other extreme right-wing/'fascist' groups in Europe at this time.

'The Nazi Party was not a fascist party'. **?** Can you explain this view of the NSDAP? Read the section on Italian Fascism and then, using the skills and knowledge that you have gained, answer this question using analysis.

Adolf Hitler, 1889–1945

The Founding of the Nazi Party: 1919–1924

In 1919 an obscure lance-corporal left a German army hospital, where he had been recovering from a mustard gas attack, outraged that civilian politicians of the new Weimar Republic had 'stabbed Germany in the back' by negotiating an armistice with the Allies. Employed by the army to spy on extreme nationalist groups in Munich, he became attracted to one of them – the German Workers' Party (DAP) – joined it and became one of its most effective speakers. When it changed its name to the National Socialist German Workers' Party (NSDAP or Nazi Party) in 1920, Adolf Hitler was one of its leading members.

ADOLF HITLER

Hitler was not a German but an Austrian, a young man who had failed to make a career for himself in Vienna before the war but who, in drifting around its streets, had picked up all kinds of prejudices that could be found there. *Pan-Germanism*, the belief that all Germans should live in one country; *social Darwinism*, the idea of the survival of the fittest race; and *anti-Semitism*, a profound hatred of the Jews and Jewish culture – all of these found their way into the mind of the young misfit. It was perhaps to get away from the cosmopolitan ideas of Vienna, and to a more disciplined life with clearly stated aims and values, that Hitler rushed to enlist in the German army in 1914, where he served with distinction throughout the war.

THE NSDAP (NAZI PARTY)

As its name suggested, the Nazi Party was meant to be both nationalist and socialist. It aimed to overthrow the Treaty of Versailles, to include all Germans in one *Reich* or state, and to exclude Jews from German citizenship; but it also proposed the introduction of profit-sharing in big business, the regulation of large department stores and the confiscation of unearned income. In addition to this programme Hitler, as propaganda chief, developed an image for the party that made it instantly recognisable: military-style uniforms, the swastika symbol and the Nazi salute. By July 1921, Hitler had established a dominant position in the party and was able to become its leader.

THE MUNICH *PUTSCH*

While the NSDAP did have branches outside southern Germany, it was in Bavaria that it was strongest, and where its party rallies and stormtroopers (the SA) were most noticeable. Nevertheless, it was only one of many small, right-wing groups there; and when, in 1923, Hitler became convinced that the hour for a national revolution had come, he needed the support of the leader of the Bavarian state government, von Kahr, and of other right-wing figures, to launch his *Putsch*. It was a fiasco. The revolt was launched in a Munich beer-hall where von Kahr was speaking, but unknown to Hitler he had had second thoughts, and with little support from the local army or police the revolt was crushed: 14 Nazis were killed and Hitler was arrested and tried for treason. He was sentenced to five years' imprisonment, but actually served only ten months in the not uncomfortable surroundings of Landsberg castle.

MEIN KAMPF

While in Landsberg prison Hitler wrote the book that was to become the bible of the Nazi Party: *Mein Kampf* or 'My Struggle'. It was a mixture of autobiography (inaccurate), early history of the party (overblown) and political theory (unoriginal), and was not so much a programme as a framework for action, yet it contained elements of everything that the Nazi state was to become. The concept of *Volk* or race was key: the *Herrenvolk* or master race were Aryan or Germanic, and superior to other races such as the Slavs or the Negroes. The Jews, spread around the world and 'infecting' all nations, were a cancer that had to be excised. The German *Volk* needed a *Reich* in which to live, one that encompassed all Germans: and should that not be big enough, then *Lebensraum*, or living-space, should be found by expanding into Poland and Russia. To lead this *Volksgemeinschaft* (people's community), a strong leader, or *Führer*, would be needed.

Adolf Hitler always considered himself to be this leader, and when he left Landsberg in December 1924 he set out to achieve his aims; but for the present he would have to wait, because not only had the Nazi Party fallen apart without his leadership during his ten months in prison, but Germany itself had changed.

Italian Fascism

'Fascism' or 'fascist' is today a term of abuse levelled against any person or government people believe to be too right-wing or dictatorial. Yet in the 1920s it meant something very different.

Fascism began in Italy in the early 1920s. Benito Mussolini, a former newspaper editor, and many of his countrymen, were alarmed at the rise of communism, angry at Italy's treatment in the Paris Peace Treaties, and scornful of the 'weak', democratic politicians who, they believed, had failed Italy.

Grouping together under Mussolini's leadership, ex-soldiers, nationalists and any thug who liked to wear a uniform formed a Fascist party and bullied their way into government in 1922, setting up a Fascist state.

The features of Fascism were:
- fierce anti-communism
- aggressive nationalism
- distrust of liberalism and democracy
- the use of propaganda and indoctrination
- a totalitarian, one-party state
- a *Duce* or leader
- a strong identity with uniforms and a military-style structure
- a belief that individuals come second to the community
- a willingness to take actions ahead of thought

Many books have been written on Hitler and the Nazi Party. Three of the best (and you should try to read at least one of these) on *Hitler* are by A. Bullock (Pelican, 1975), J. Fest (Harcourt Brace Jovanovich, 1992) and I. Kershaw (Longman, 1991). The text of Hitler's book *Mein Kampf* is available in an English translation (Pimlico, 1992).

A stormtrooper of the SA

Hitler used the SA under Röhm to help forge the power base of the Nazi Party, but later feared that they would lead a 'second revolution' and removed the threat in The Night of the Long Knives

It would be very easy here to make enough notes to write a book. Try to confine yourself to Hitler's Background; his role as Party Leader; the importance of The Munich *Putsch*; and the essence of Hitler's Ideas.

THE KEY ISSUE

Were the middle years of the Weimar Republic as stable and prosperous as they appeared?

THE KEY SKILLS

Interpretation
Assessment

WHAT YOU HAVE TO DO

Use the Key Issue as a question. Use the skills that you have and the evidence that you have gathered to assess the stability and prosperity of Weimar Germany from 1924 to 1929.

Weimar and the Rise of Hitler by A. Nicholls (Macmillan, 1991).

Was the stability and prosperity of Weimar Germany from 1924 to 1929 real; relative to what had gone before; or was it superficial, apparent on the surface but based on an illusion? **?**

German Prosperity, Economic Problems, Political Instability and the years of Nazi Marginalisation. Remember that the main thing you are looking to do when you read your books is to *gather evidence* about the stability and prosperity (real or apparent) of the middle years of the Weimar Republic.

The Middle Years of Weimar: 1924–1929

In the years 1924–1929, the Weimar Republic appeared to achieve stability, growth and prosperity. Inflation was checked, industry was rebuilt and reorganised, and exports rose. More and better schools and houses were built, wages rose, and people bought more cars and other consumer goods. Support for the nationalists and the Nazis fell, and swung towards those political parties who had always supported the Republic. Under Stresemann, foreign minister for six years, the Dawes Plan was accepted, French troops left the Ruhr and the Locarno treaties were signed in 1925. Germany was admitted to the League of Nations as a permanent member of the Council in 1926, and in 1929 Germany signed the Kellogg–Briand Pact, and acceded to the Young Plan, whereby reparations were reduced by 75% and agreed to be paid over a 60-year period. Germany was once again accepted as an equal by the other great powers, and took her place on the world stage; but the apparent economic prosperity and political stability hid unpalatable facts.

UNDERLYING ECONOMIC AND POLITICAL PROBLEMS

Germany could only afford to repay reparations to the Allies, chiefly Britain and France, because of American loans; and Britain and France relied on German reparations to repay their war debts to America. Consequently, if the Americans ever withdrew their loans, the whole financial merry-go-round would collapse. American loans, attracted to Germany by high interest rates, were also bankrolling German companies: if the loans were to be withdrawn, many German businesses would be likely to close.

The growth of the German economy was erratic in these years: unemployment was never less than 1 million, and more than 70 million working days were lost through strike action. Workers were paid more, but often had to work harder, and for longer hours. Farmers and their families (one-third of the population) did not share in this prosperity, as changing economic conditions led to a fall in world food prices, and consequently a decline in their income. There was also little home-grown saving, Germans preferring to spend their money.

While votes for extremist parties declined, political stability did not increase. The fragmentation of the parties led to shifting coalitions between them: in the years between 1923 and 1930 there were no fewer than seven different governments, and only one of these was led by the largest party in the *Reichstag*, the SPD. The coalitions were all different combinations of the centre-left or centre-right, as communists and nationalists refused to join them. Moreover, the election of Hindenburg in 1925 signalled a nationalist, right-wing President, not known to be sympathetic to the Republic.

HITLER AND THE NAZI PARTY

Hitler refounded the Nazi Party in 1925, although it took him a year to overcome internal differences and regional hostilities before he was once again the unquestioned *Führer*. Believing now that the only way to gain power was by legal means, he set about creating a new party structure. Germany was divided into *Gaue*, or regions, each run by a *Gauleiter*, who ran the party there, and reported directly to Hitler. Other organisations – the Hitler Youth, the Nazi Teachers' Association and the SS – were also set up as semi-independent bodies, again responsible to Hitler. In this way, Nazi ideas were spread into different areas, with Hitler as the sole unifying force. Party membership increased, and other extreme right-wing groups were absorbed, but the party still only managed 2.6% of the vote in the 1928 elections.

This result, however, was not as bad as it first seemed. The Nazi vote was very uneven across Germany, and in the farming areas of the north and west, suffering from the agricultural depression, it was as high as 10% in some places. This protest vote, going to the Nazis rather than to other parties, was seen as a pointer to the future. Then, three weeks after accepting the Young Plan on behalf of Germany at the Reparations Conference at the Hague, Stresemann died. That same month, October 1929, saw the Wall Street Crash, the start of the withdrawal of American loans from Germany, and the onset of the Great Depression. It marked the beginning of the transformation of the Nazi Party into a mass party of protest.

Reichstag election results in the Weimar Republic: 1919–1932

Seats won by the major parties at each election

Party	1919	1920	1924	1924	1928	1930	1932	1932
KPD	—	4	62	45	54	77	89	100
USPD	22	84	—	—	—	—	—	—
SPD	165	102	100	131	153	143	133	121
DDP	75	39	28	32	25	20	4	2
Zentrum/BVP	91	85	81	88	78	87	97	90
DVP	19	65	45	51	45	30	7	11
DNVP	44	71	95	103	73	41	37	52
NSDAP	—	—	32	14	12	107	230	196
Others	7	9	29	29	51	72	11	12

Evidence

Evidence does not always confirm what historians write: sometimes it appears to contradict it. For example, below are two accounts of the middle years of Weimar Germany that seem to give a completely different view to the one I have given. Am I wrong, are they, or is there a more subtle answer?

One view of the prosperity of the Weimar Republic

'Between 1924 and 1929 German industry forged ahead. Factories were equipped with new machinery and German industrialists used the most successful techniques of American production. These were assembly lines, standardised patterns and interchangeable parts, all of which enabled goods to be mass-produced. The result was a much faster economic growth rate than either Britain or France. By 1929 Germany was producing 33% more than it had done in 1913, despite losing its major industrial areas under the Treaty of Versailles.'
Stephen Lee, Weimar and Nazi Germany, 1996

One view of the stability of the Weimar Republic

'Life seemed more free, more modern, more exciting than in any place I had ever seen. Nowhere else did the arts or the intellectual life seem so lively ... The old, oppressive Prussian spirit seemed to be dead and buried. Most Germans one met – politicians, writers, editors, artists, professors, students, businessmen, labour leaders – struck you as being liberal, democratic, even pacifist.'
William L. Shirer, Berlin Diary, 1941

THE KEY ISSUES

- Why did the Great Depression hit Weimar Germany so hard?
- Why did the fortunes of the Nazi Party rise so dramatically in the 1930 election?

THE KEY SKILLS

Explanation
Interpretation
Empathy

WHAT YOU HAVE TO DO

Use the Key Issues as questions and try to explain the depth of the Great Depression in Germany. Investigate the Nazi Party machine and its propaganda, and try to empathise with the German voters in 1930.

I. Kershaw (ed.), *Weimar: Why did German Democracy Fail?* (Weidenfeld and Nicolson, 1990); D. Muhlberger, *Hitler's Followers* (Routledge, 1991); T. Childers, *The Nazi Voter* (University of North Carolina Press, 1983).

Use the subheadings in the text and find further examples of The Effects of the Great Depression on Germany; the problems of The Politics of Deadlock and the reasons for The Growth of the Nazi Vote.

The Crisis of the Weimar Republic: 1929–1930

THE GREAT DEPRESSION

The Wall Street Crash marked the beginning of the end for the Weimar Republic. As the world lurched into economic crisis, Germany was particularly badly hit. American loans, which underpinned not only German industry but also reparations repayments, dried up; and loans previously given were demanded back. As industries began to contract, imports of raw materials and food declined: and lower prices for these products led to their producers being unable to afford manufactured goods, so export markets collapsed and world trade diminished. As industries closed in Germany bankruptcies rose, prices and wages fell, and unemployment began to increase alarmingly. Within 12 months of the Crash unemployment had doubled to 3 million, and the numbers would double again to over 6 million by 1933.

The Depression hit every sector of the German economy. Industrial workers were laid off in millions, with no prospect of finding future employment; farmers, faced with falling food prices, saw only poverty and ruin; small shopkeepers found their trade cut in half; professionals discovered that their services were no longer wanted; even large banks were forced to close, unable to meet their creditors' demands. At the height of the crisis, one in three workers was unemployed, and industrial production had nearly halved:

'In the relative prosperity of today it is difficult to appreciate the scale of the economic and social suffering which struck Germany in the early 1930's. To many ordinary respectable Germans it must have seemed as if society itself was breaking down uncontrollably. One-third of the population was on the dole; the city of Cologne could not pay the interest on its debts; banks closed their doors; and in Berlin large crowds of unemployed youngsters were kept occupied with open-air games of chess and cards! In such a situation it is perhaps not surprising that people lost faith in the Weimar Republic and saw salvation in the solutions offered by political extremism.'

G. Layton, From Bismarck to Hitler: Germany 1890–1933, 1995

POLITICAL DEADLOCK

The coalition that had governed Germany since 1928 found itself unable to agree on measures to deal with the crisis, and broke up in 1930. A new government, led by Brüning of the Centre Party, was formed, but found itself unable to get its proposals passed except by presidential decree. With deadlock in the *Reichstag*, Brüning called an election, hoping for the support of the people for his centre-right coalition. However, believing that the Weimar system had failed them, this being only the latest in a series of disasters that had struck Germany since 1918, many Germans began to look for an escape from the crisis by turning to parties untainted by the failures of the Republic.

THE RISE OF THE NAZI PARTY

The collapse of the Weimar Republic was paralleled by the rise of the Nazi Party. The NSDAP was in better shape in 1929 than its tiny vote of 1928 might indicate. It had 100 000 members, a strong party organisation, a ruthless and tireless leader, a clear identity and had developed sophisticated propaganda techniques for winning support. Chief among these was the way in which the Nazis targeted specific groups of voters, rather than appealing for general support among Germans as a whole. To peasant farmers, the Nazis promised relief from agricultural poverty; to small shopkeepers, protection from the large department stores; to women, a return to family values; to big business, a reduction in trade union power; to workers, jobs. Although many of these promises could be seen as contradictory, by dressing them up in themes of nationalism and morality, and by careful campaigning at a local level, the incompatibility of these promises could be camouflaged or avoided.

THE 1930 ELECTIONS

The effectiveness of these policies was seen in 1930, when the Nazis made huge gains in the *Reichstag* elections. Peasant farmers and landowners in Protestant areas, the self-employed and white-collar workers in the towns, manual workers in small industries and handicrafts, many women, and young people who had not voted before – these people turned to the Nazi Party to save them from the 'disaster' of the Weimar Republic. The Nazis gained 107 seats with nearly 20% of the vote, and established themselves as a mainstream political force. Yet large sections of the population did not vote for them. Where people were already in existing organisations, they stayed loyal to them: industrial workers in trades unions still voted for the SPD or KPD; in areas where the Catholic church was strong the Zentrum/BVP vote held steady; and the Nazis gained little support from the working class in large cities.

The Nazis and the 1930 election

'In the election campaign ... the Nazis used every trick of propaganda to attract attention and win votes. In the big towns there was a marked increase in public disorder in which the S.A. took a prominent part. Slogans painted on walls, posters, demonstrations, rallies, mass-meetings, crude and unrestrained demagogy, anything that would help to create an impression of energy, determination and success was pressed into use. Hitler's appeal in the towns was especially to the middle-class hit by the depression ... At the same time the Nazis devoted much time and attention to the rural voter ...'

A. Bullock, Hitler, 1962

Why one middle-class architect joined the Nazi Party

'Here it seemed to me was hope. Here were new ideals, a new understanding, new tasks ... The perils of Communism, which seemed inexorably on the way, could be checked, Hitler persuaded us, and instead of hopeless unemployment, Germany could move towards economic recovery. He had mentioned the Jewish problem only peripherally.'

Albert Speer, Inside the Third Reich, 1995

How Nazi propaganda worked

'The issues deployed by Nazi electoral propaganda to mobilise ... support were many and various. Of these almost all commentators agree that the most significant were nationalism, the denunciation of the Treaty of Versailles, and anti-Marxism, though it should be noted that this last meant opposition not only to the Communists, but also to the SPD, the unions, labour law and welfare legislation.'

Dick Geary, Hitler and Nazism, 1993

THE KEY ISSUES

- To what extent did 'presidential government' lead to the downfall of the Weimar Republic?
- Was the Weimar Republic inherently weak, and did this contribute to the rise of the Nazis?

THE KEY SKILLS

Assessment
Explanation
Interpretation

WHAT YOU HAVE TO DO

Using the evidence that you have, you should try to answer the questions posed by the Key Issues. Try to assess the relative importance of presidential government, backstairs intrigue and lack of majority coalitions in the period 1930–1932 and decide what it was that ultimately led to the downfall of Weimar Germany.

Was the Weimar Republic? similar to or different from other European states of the time?

The Collapse of the Weimar Republic by D. Abraham (Holmes & Meier, 1986). Note that A. Bullock's *Hitler* looks in depth at the backstairs intrigues that brought Hitler to power.

The Government of Brüning, the Two Elections in 1932 and the Backstairs Intrigues that brought Hitler to power. Also try to read about the history of other European countries in the 1920s and 1930s, and make notes on their similarities to the Weimar Republic.

The Fall of the Weimar Republic: 1930–1933

PRESIDENTIAL GOVERNMENT: BRÜNING

Brüning remained as Chancellor from 1930 to 1932. In office he raised taxes and cut spending, which only worsened the effects of the Depression; but his determination, to show that Germany could no longer afford to pay reparations, worked, for these were abolished by the Lausanne Conference in June 1932. Yet he was only able to govern by using the special provision of Article 48 of the Weimar Constitution, which enabled laws to be signed by presidential decree, for he headed a minority coalition. There were, in fact, no more majority governments: democracy in the Weimar Republic ended in 1930, for after that date no coalition could be formed that would command the support of the *Reichstag*, and the cabinets supported by Hindenburg were regularly outvoted in Parliament.

One of Brüning's last acts was to secure the re-election of Hindenburg as President. The old man had served out his seven-year term, but was persuaded to stand again because of the general state of the country. He was opposed by Hitler and a Communist candidate, but won with an absolute majority of the vote. Nevertheless, the Nazis had fought a very effective campaign, raising their profile. Hindenburg, now surrounded by and influenced by a group of people that included his son, aristocrats and army officers, was persuaded to sack Brüning and replace him with an aristocrat, Papen, who formed a cabinet of landowners and industrialists who were looking to bring in a corporate state.

THE JULY 1932 ELECTION

The *Reichstag* was dissolved and fresh elections were called for July 1932. The campaign was marked by violence, as the SA and the SS clashed with communist and socialist groups in some vicious street-fighting that left over 100 dead. It was also marked by new levels of political sophistication as Hitler, backed by money from industrialists, made flights and speaking engagements all over Germany and used every kind of device – music, flags, posters and mass rallies – to raise the awareness of the voter. The Nazis made large gains from Protestant and middle-class parties and doubled their vote to over 13.7 million, or 37.3%, giving them 230 seats in the *Reichstag* and making them the largest party.

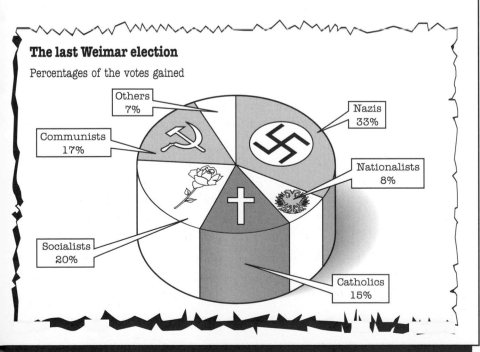

PRESIDENTIAL GOVERNMENT: PAPEN AND SCHLEICHER

Hitler now determined to accept nothing less than the chancellorship, and he was unwilling to enter any coalition; but as long as Papen had the ear of Hindenburg, he was powerless. Papen, anxious to undermine the Nazis, and believing that they had reached their peak, now called further elections for November: and this time the Nazi vote fell to under 12 million, or 33.1%, and they lost 34 seats. However, the army had by now lost confidence in Papen, and their political voice, Major-General Schleicher, persuaded Hindenburg to withdraw his support from Papen, and install himself as Chancellor instead.

The last days of the Weimar Republic were played out to backstairs intrigue. Schleicher aimed to create a broad-based government by detatching the left wing of the Nazi Party and persuading it to join with the SPD, but failed. Papen, aiming to return to government, had secret meetings with Hitler to form a nationalist–Nazi coalition, and persuaded industrialists and landowners to back him against what they saw as Schleicher's dangerous games. Hindenburg, believing that the Nazis in government would be 'tamed' by the nationalists and conservatives, withdrew his support from Schleicher, and on 30 January 1933 appointed Adolf Hitler as Chancellor of a coalition government.

The conservative elites, which Papen and Hindenburg represented, not the electorate, determined that Hitler should come to power in Germany. Had the politicians of the left and centre worked together they could have formed a credible parliamentary alternative, but the Communists were waiting for the revolution, and the socialists and Catholics had too little in common. As it was, they were soon all to be swept away in the Nazi tide that was set to engulf the country.

The last Weimar election

Percentages of the votes gained

Others 7%
Communists 17%
Socialists 20%
Nazis 33%
Nationalists 8%
Catholics 15%

Weimar Germany in European history

After 1945, many people tried to explain the history of Germany in the 20th century in terms of a *Sonderweg*; that is, a special path of development that turned Germany on to a course that led directly to two world wars. People blamed Prussian militarism, a lack of liberalism, conservative elites, the ideas of Nietzsche, and especially the Weimar Republic for the emergence of Hitler and the Nazis.

Yet the Weimar Republic was typical of European states in the inter-war years. Both Britain and France had the same political instability as Weimar, similar industrial unrest and rising unemployment in the 1930s. Only Germany suffered hyperinflation, but Britain had to come off the gold standard in 1931, and the French franc was devalued in 1928 and 1936.

Hitler only came to power in Germany a decade after Mussolini in Italy. In Britain, MacDonald of Labour was forced into a coalition with Liberals and Conservatives in 1931; while the French fascist leagues had over half a million members by 1936, and only an alliance of radicals, socialists and communists in a Popular Front was able to stop them from destroying democracy.

Many of the problems that the Weimar Republic faced were European in nature, not strictly German; while the greatest problem of all, the Great Depression, was essentially a failure of American capitalism. The Weimar Republic has been unfairly blamed.

THE KEY ISSUE

How were the Nazis able to establish, and then consolidate, a dictatorship in Germany within 18 months of coming to power?

THE KEY SKILLS

Explanation
Analysis
Chronology

WHAT YOU HAVE TO DO

This is one part of your study when you really do need to know in some detail not only the events that happened but the order in which they took place as well. It would not be out of place in this section to make a chronological table or flowchart – NOT a timeline, but a step-by-step guide to the events of this period, including a detailed breakdown of the effects of what took place.

The best account of this period is in I. Kershaw's *Hitler* (Longman, 1991); but you could also look at F. Tobias' *The Reichstag Fire* (Secker & Warburg, 1963) or, for a look at the experience of a single town, W. S. Allen, *The Nazi Seizure of Power* (Penguin, 1989).

This chapter is one of the few where the 'how' is more important than the 'why'. To that extent your notes should be more of a narrative nature than in most sections. A great deal happened in The First Two Months of Nazi Rule; and A National Revolution followed in the period to August 1934. The Second Revolution (see opposite) was something that never happened, but it nevertheless had important consequences for the way the Nazi state developed.

The Nazi Seizure of Power: 1933–1934

When Adolf Hitler became Chancellor of Germany on 30 January 1933, he was one of only three Nazis in a coalition cabinet: yet within weeks the Nazi Party had taken control of the country. Hitler's first act was to call for another election, which in his mind was to be Germany's last. Using presidential decrees, he then gained the power to forbid political meetings and ban newspapers, and dissolved the Prussian Parliament, giving Göring (the Nazi Minister of the Interior for Prussia, the largest of Germany's federal states), effective control of 60% of Germany's police who, bolstered by 50 000 SA men, were then ordered to work to support the Nazi Party! A programme of legalised terror against the SPD and the KPD ensued, culminating in Nazi reaction to the *Reichstag* fire (supposedly burnt down by a Dutch communist) when the 'Decree for the Protection of the People and State' was passed, which allowed the government to arrest people at will, and even take over provincial governments. Hundreds of communists and socialists were arrested, and intimidation reached new heights. In spite of this, the Nazis still won under 44% of the votes, and could only claim a majority in Parliament with the support of the nationalists.

THE ENABLING ACT

In many Catholic and working-class areas of Germany the Nazis suffered heavy defeats, but this did not stop their drive for power. They simply seized control of state governments; and then, to entrench their power nationally, demanded an Enabling Act, giving Hitler and his government full powers for four years. On 23 March, with Communist deputies excluded and SA and SS stormtroopers lining the walls, the ZP was persuaded to join the Nazis and nationalists in voting for the Act and, with only the socialists voting against it, Hitler got the two-thirds majority that he needed to pass it. The way to a legal dictatorship was now open.

'Outside in the square the huge crowd roared its approval. The Nazis had every reason to be delighted: with the passage of the Enabling Act, Hitler secured his independence, not only from the Reichstag but also from the President. The earlier Chancellors, Brüning, Papen and Schleicher, had all been dependent on the President's power to issue emergency decrees under Article 48 of the Constitution: now Hitler had that right for himself, with full power to set aside the Constitution. The street gangs had seized control of the resources of a great modern State, the gutter had come to power.'

Alan Bullock, Hitler, 1962

THE LEGAL REVOLUTION

Hitler now moved to bring the country into line (the *Gleichschaltung*) with the Nazi Party. Provincial state governments were brought under the control of Nazi-appointed Reich governors, and their parliaments were later abolished. Trade union power had already been emasculated by the Depression, but on 2 May (after a Nazi-inspired holiday) their offices were raided and occupied, their leaders arrested, and their organisations absorbed into a new German Labour Front. It was impossible to conceive of other political parties coexisting with the Nazis, so the KPD and the SPD were banned, and all other parties dissolved themselves. Schools and universities were forced to introduce new syllabuses, and teachers and lecturers had to belong to Nazi-dominated organisations. German businesses were brought under a Reich Economic Chamber. Writers and artists were forced to join a Reich Chamber of Culture. Life in Germany was deliberately Nazified.

THE NIGHT OF THE LONG KNIVES

One of the few areas of German life not 'brought into line' was the army: Hitler needed it as his guarantor of power. Yet there was a rival military force that believed that it had brought Hitler to power: the 2 million men of the SA, led by Röhm, the street-fighters who tended to be on the left wing of the party, and who were now looking to Hitler to make them the vanguard of a Second Revolution, as a people's army. The army had no wish to see itself displaced by the SA: other Nazi leaders feared Röhm's power; and it was clear by the spring of 1934 that Hindenburg had little time left to live. To secure his personal position, get rid of Röhm, and gain the support of the generals, Hitler decided to eliminate the threat from the SA.

On 30 June, 1934 Röhm, and about 400 leaders of the SA, were murdered in 'The Night of the Long Knives' by the SS, with army support. In addition, Hitler took the opportunity to settle old scores, having Schleicher, the former Chancellor, and Strasser, leader of the left wing of the Nazi Party, killed. This action cleared the way for Hitler's personal supremacy: when Hindenburg died on 2 August, Hitler combined the offices of Chancellor and President to become *Führer*. When, on the same day, every soldier swore an oath of personal loyalty to him, Hitler became leader of the party, the army and the nation.

The 'Second Revolution'

The Nazi Party brought a political and social revolution to Germany: but there were many within its ranks who wanted an economic revolution as well.

While it is true that the bulk of the industrial workers had never supported the policies of the Nazi Party, the Nazis had attracted a sizeable working-class following that tended to be populist, left-wing and anti-capitalist. These people believed in the 'socialist' element of the party's programme, and many of them had joined the SA, had won the political battles on the streets against the communists, and now looked to be rewarded by a true 'National Socialist Revolution' as outlined by their leader, Ernst Röhm. They wanted big business, the army and all the conservative elements of the German establishment swept away, and their replacement by something 'new, fresh, unused and revolutionary', as Röhm wanted.

Röhm was one of Hitler's oldest comrades, and the SA a force of committed Nazis; but Hitler had been brought to power by the conservative elites of Germany (who hated Röhm and his ideas) and he needed them, for the moment at least, to stay in power. Hitler also had no interest in economics, and was determined that the Nazi revolution was to be imposed from above, not dictated from below. The 'National Revolution', which he was busily pushing through, had happened; there was no need for, and many potential dangers in, a second one.

Ultimately, Röhm alive was much more of a threat to Hitler than the consequences of Röhm dead; and by killing Röhm and other leaders of the SA, the threat of a 'Second Revolution' vanished.

THE KEY ISSUES

- To what extent was Hitler the supreme leader of the Nazi state?
- To what extent was Nazi Germany organised along totalitarian lines?

THE KEY SKILLS

Explanation
Assessment

WHAT YOU HAVE TO DO

The Key Issues may seem to state the obvious; but if you have read this section, or done some other research, it should be clear that they pose genuine problems. If you can go some way towards explaining Hitler's position as *Führer*, and how the Nazi state was organised, then you will be breaking a few well-established myths.

How different were the character of Hitler, and of the Nazi state, from the myths of popular perception? **?**

The chaotic nature of the Third Reich is best summarised in I. Kershaw's *Hitler* (Longman, 1991); and the leading figures of Nazi Germany are well drawn in J. Fest's *The Face of the Third Reich* (Penguin, 1979).

Find out more about Hitler's lieutenants, the people he surrounded himself with and who took charge of the different areas of Nazi Germany. Find out more about The Nazi Party from 1933 and its effects upon German life.

The Extension of Nazi Rule: 1933–1945

HITLER AS *FÜHRER*

The Nazi state came into being because of Adolf Hitler: yet while Hitler was *Führer* and the supreme arbiter of policy it is wrong to think of him as leader in any dynamic sense. Hitler played little part in day-to-day policy: detail seems to have bored him, and he was reluctant to take decisions, often preferring to let things work themselves out. He rarely appeared before lunch, and would often spend his afternoons taking walks or watching films. He might spend days considering a problem, then resolve it with a burst of energy, only to relax back into inactivity again. Yet he retained supreme power because he was the ultimate source of authority: his underlings might rule their empires, but everything was done in his name.

THE NAZI PARTY AND THE STATE

Nazi Germany was not the monolithic, totalitarian state that its propaganda made it out to be. Unlike Soviet Russia, the party did not control every aspect of life: rather, it attached itself to institutions, supervised them or worked in parallel with them. For example, the German Civil Service was an efficient, professional and conservative body, and although it was purged of Jews in 1933, it was largely left alone until 1939, when new entrants had to be party members. The Foreign Office continued to exist, although various Nazi foreign 'bureaux' shadowed and sometimes duplicated its work.

The two organisations that seemed likely to remain free of interference in the Nazi state were the church and the army: both had long traditions of independence and both seemed strong enough to resist Nazism. Yet almost at once the Nazis began to persecute and harass the churches inside Germany, undermining the clergy, attacking church property and rejecting Christian values. However, this policy of attrition never succeeded in changing the beliefs of a majority of Germans. Hitler had needed the support of the army in 1934, and left it alone while it was rearming; but the reluctance of the generals to back him over his foreign policy adventures convinced him of their spineless nature, and he sacked their leaders and became Commander-in-Chief himself in 1938. From then on, the influence of the army was much reduced and it loyally took its orders – until defeats in 1943 and 1944 spurred some of its members to try to kill Hitler. The failure of this plot ended its independent position, and by the end of the war it had been brought effectively under the control of the SS.

Nazi Germany

The different organisations that made up Nazi Germany were like competing empires. Schacht, the Minister of Economics, was virtually an economic dictator from 1934, and yet found himself in conflict with – and then pushed out by – Göring, whose own Office of the Four Year Plan was set up, and then expanded, from 1936. Göring himself then came into conflict with Todt, the Armaments Minister, from 1940 onwards. Goebbels, the Propaganda Minister, first brought radio and the press under his control, and then extended his influence into film, music, literature and art. Schirach ran the Hitler Youth as his personal fief.

The greatest empire builder was, however, Himmler. Leader of the SS since 1929, he created the party's own security service, the SD, in 1931; gained control of the *Gestapo* in 1934; and by 1936 was chief of all German police. Over the years the SS became responsible for all security matters, ran the concentration camps, formed its own military wing (the *Waffen* SS), ran the 'New Order' in eastern Europe, and developed its own industrial complexes, using prisoners of war and slave labour. By 1945 it had become a state within a state.

The Supremacy of Hitler

Nazi Germany was perhaps the supreme example of a *chaotic* state. All of the organisations referred to above, and others such as the party *Gaue*, the Labour Front, and the various Nazi trade and professional groups, were effectively independent of each other: they followed their own interests, had only vaguely defined areas of responsibility, and were constantly trying to extend their authority. These 'power blocs' did not work in unison, or under a hierarchy of control: instead, each of their leaders reported directly to Hitler, and wielded power under his authority alone. The myth that Nazi Germany was a disciplined, efficient, totalitarian state, with formal chains of command extending in a rigid pyramid from Hitler down, is just that – a myth. Hitler was supreme as *Führer*, and no person could challenge his authority; but beneath him his lieutenants feuded with, intrigued against and clashed with each other. It was divide and rule.

'When, I would often ask myself, did he really work? Little was left of the day; he rose late in the morning and conducted one or two official conferences; but from the subsequent dinner on he more or less wasted his time until the early hours of the evening. His rare appointments in the late afternoon were imperilled by his passion for looking at building plans.

The adjutants often asked me: "Please don't show any plans today". Then the drawings I had brought with me would be left by the telephone switchboard at the entrance and I would reply evasively to Hitler's enquiries. Sometimes he would see through this game and would himself go to look in the anteroom or the cloakroom for my roll of plans.'

Albert Speer, Hitler's architect, from Inside the Third Reich, 1995

Heinrich Himmler, Reichsführer SS

A sadistic chicken-farmer from Bavaria, he joined the Nazis in 1923 and rose through their ranks until he was selected in 1929 to command the SS (*Schutzstaffeln*). He transformed this black-shirted elite from a few dozen men who comprised Hitler's personal bodyguard into a vast organisation of hundreds of thousands. He had sole power over the whole structure of the police state; he ruled all of the SS organisations; and by 1944 was C-in-C of the German Home Army.

He also believed unquestioningly in the racist doctrines of the Nazi Party. He set up SS institutes for the study of heredity; he was passionately interested in all aspects of Aryan 'culture'; he believed absolutely in Nordic 'supremacy'; and he was personally happy to assume control of the Final Solution and take responsibility for ridding Europe of Jews.

By 1945 his power was second only to Hitler's, and he was the most feared man in Germany. But he did not stand trial for his crimes: arrested after the war by British troops, dressed as an army corporal, he committed suicide by taking poison two days later.

THE KEY ISSUES

- To what extent did the Nazis turn round the German economy?
- To what extent did the various social classes in Germany benefit from a Nazi economy?

THE KEY SKILLS

Interpretation
Assessment

WHAT YOU HAVE TO DO

It is quite difficult to tackle the Key Issues, because you have to consider both real and apparent effects of Nazi policies. For example, W. L. Shirer writes of everyone being 'as busy as a bee' in the Nazi era, and huge numbers of people were employed, many in new industries: but were they producing real goods, or were they doing the modern equivalent of digging holes in the ground only to fill them up again?

German agriculture

The Hereditary Farm Law of 1933 declared that all farms up to 125 hectares were 'hereditary estates' which could not be sold, divided or foreclosed for debts. On the death of the owner they had to be passed to the nearest male relative; and only an Aryan German who could prove his ancestry back to 1800 could own such a farm.

The Reich Food Estate, established in 1933, fixed farm prices at a profitable level, oversaw all branches of agricultural production, marketing and processing, and succeeded in raising German food production to 83% of the level needed for self-sufficiency.

Employment and the Economy: 1933–1939

Mass unemployment had been one of the causes of the downfall of the Weimar Republic, but Nazi Germany could claim to have cured it, the jobless figure falling from 6 million in 1933 to 300 000 six years later. Yet, to Hitler, economics came a poor third to politics and military matters: so how was this achieved? First, public works: by drafting young unemployed men into the German Labour Service to build *autobahns* and plant forests, a million people could be taken off the unemployment lists. Second, by cutting imports and boosting exports wherever possible, jobs were created by regenerating trade. Third, by following a policy of 'autarky': becoming self-sufficient in key raw materials such as oil, metals and rubber, the coal, steel and electrochemicals industries were vastly increased, new processes to produce synthetic substitutes were developed, and thousands of new jobs were created. Fourth, by rearmament: investing billions of *Reichsmarks* in the research, development and production of weapons of war gave jobs to tens of thousands in the aircraft, shipbuilding, armaments and explosives industries. Fifth, conscription: by compulsory military service and a huge expansion in the armed forces after 1935, another half a million young men were 'called up'.

These figures, however, point to the artificial nature of the new employment. Only a fraction of these new jobs were due to the expansion of a normal peacetime economy: all of the others were due to the creation of an economy geared up for war and conquest. Moreover, certain classes of people – Jews, some married women, 'political' prisoners in concentration camps and so on – disappeared from the unemployment registers for ideological reasons. The Nazis claimed to have eliminated unemployment, but only because they had created a distorted economic system.

THE GERMAN WORKFORCE

To many Germans, however, it seemed as though the Nazis had turned the economy around, and the material benefits could be considerable. A weekly wage was now coming in for almost all families; the 'Beauty of Labour' organisation (SDA) did improve working conditions for many; and the 'Strength Through Joy' movement (KDF) provided cultural, sporting and leisure activities outside the workplace. However, workers had lost their trade union and bargaining rights, and had to work longer hours for lower real wages, as the Nazis gave preferential treatment to the owners of factories, rather than their workforces.

The German Labour Front, under Ley, was created in 1934 to replace the old trades unions, but it encompassed employers and professional organisations as well. Far from protecting the rights of workers, its aim was 'to see that every single individual should be able ... to perform the maximum of work'.

Wages tended to be set at rates the employers wanted, and were kept low. Taxes and contributions took up to 35% of a worker's pay. Every worker had to have a 'work-book' which went with him from job to job: but if his employer kept it, he could not legally be employed elsewhere.

The Labour Front did provide sporting and leisure activities through its KDF movement: it organised cheap holidays, and had two cruise liners and even its own orchestra; but the workers had to pay their dues to it, and its greatest scam, the Volkswagen, brought in tens of millions of marks – and not one car was ever delivered!

THE PEASANTRY

For the peasants the influence of Nazi Germany was also mixed. The Nazis saw them as the purest element of the *Volk*, and protected them by passing laws giving security of tenure, by reviving peasant folklore and by ensuring that food prices rose. However, these laws also meant bureaucratic interference in the way that farms were run, and forbade the break-up of holdings, which meant that only one male child could inherit a farm from his parents. This, and the attractions of towns, where wages were higher and opportunities greater, led to a growing drift away from the land.

THE MIDDLE CLASSES

Nor did the middle classes of Germany necessarily benefit from Nazi rule. Small shopkeepers were helped when large taxes were imposed on department stores and no new ones were allowed to be built; and artisans and craftsmen benefited from increased orders and sales from the general economic recovery. Germany could not become a great military power on the products of artisans, however, and it was big business rather than small – the large firms and great industrial combines – that gained most from the policies of rearmament and autarky that the Nazis implemented.

. R. Gillingham's
*ndustry and Politics
1 the Third Reich*
Methuen, 1985) and, for a
iew of agriculture under
ie Nazis, *The Plough and
ie Swastika* by J. G.
arquharson (Sage, 1976).

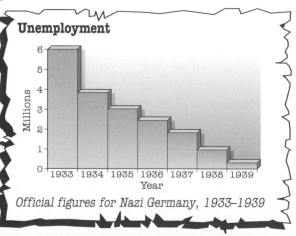

Official figures for Nazi Germany, 1933–1939

'We in Germany have really broken with a world of prejudices. I leave myself out of account. I too am a child of the people; I do not trace my line from any castle: I come from the workshop. Nor was I a general: I was simply a soldier, as were millions of others ... By my side stand Germans from all walks of life who today are amongst the leaders of the nation: men who were once workers on the land are now governing German states in the name of the Reich ... It is true that men who came from the bourgeoisie [middle classes] and former aristocrats have their place in this movement. But to us it matters nothing whence they come if only they can work to the profit of our people. That is the decisive test. We have not broken down classes in order to set new ones in their place: we have broken down classes in order to make way for the German people as a whole.'

From a speech by Adolf Hitler in Berlin, 1937

Were the people of Germany really better off under Nazi rule when many were very tightly controlled by the state?

You really need to consider two main headings here: The German Economy in its overall sense, considering industry, investment and unemployment; and you also need to think about the effect of all this on The Different Social Classes, and how each of these responded.

THE KEY ISSUE

How did the Nazis change the way of life of the German people between 1933 and 1939?

THE KEY SKILLS

Empathy
Explanation
Investigation

WHAT YOU HAVE TO DO

Try to answer the Key Issue. You must try to 'get inside' or empathise with the people of Nazi Germany, and you can do this through examining sources from those who lived in Germany at this time. You must explain what the Nazis did to change German life, and how these changes affected different groups of people.

For a general view of life in Nazi Germany, you could read *A Social History of the Third Reich* by R. Grunberger (Penguin, 1991). For women, see *Mothers in the Fatherland: Women, the Family and Nazi Politics* by C. Koonz (Methuen, 1988); and for German Youth and Social Outcasts see the chapters in *Life in the Third Reich* by R. Bessel (ed.) (Oxford University Press, 1987). If you want to see the effect of propaganda in the Nazi state, try to watch one of the films of Leni Riefenstahl: an outstanding director, she portrays the Nazi state with great visual power and imagery.

Use the subheadings within these pages. As we are only just beginning to understand the effects that the Nazis had on these groups, there is scope for you to find out more about one or all of the classes of people mentioned.

People and Culture: 1933–1939

YOUNG PEOPLE

The Nazis put great emphasis on shaping and indoctrinating the youth of Germany: liberal ideas were rejected, and were replaced by a rigid ideology. A centralised Reich Ministry of Education and Science took control of schools and reshaped the curriculum. Physical education was moved from the periphery to the centre; History, German and Biology became core subjects; and any Jewish influence, such as that of Einstein in Physics, was removed. Teachers were screened, and had to belong to the NS Teachers' League. Different types of elite school for boys and young men, emphasising physical and political education, and paramilitary activities, were set up.

This reorganisation of education was complemented by a huge growth in the Nazi youth movement outside school. Divided into different age groups, and with separate organisations for boys and girls, the Hitler Youth dressed in uniforms and were regimented along paramilitary lines; they went on summer camps and engaged in endless physical activities; boys were taught to shoot, sail or fly, and girls to cook, clean and be good mothers; great emphasis was given to competition, and to political indoctrination. Many young people enjoyed these activities: others did all they could to avoid them.

WOMEN

Nazi ideology stressed that women had a different role to that of men: as a man was a warrior and provider, so a woman was a mother and home-maker; and this dogma excluded women from the workplace and politics and tied them to the house. In practice, however, millions of German women worked, and were starting to have smaller families. Attempts to reverse this process were made: married women were debarred from some of the professions, employers were advised positively to discriminate in favour of men, strict anti-abortion laws were passed, and propaganda campaigns were made and honours and rewards given in favour of mothers. The birth rate increased, and the proportion of women in paid employment did initially fall; yet the growth in the German economy created many more job opportunities for women, and by 1939 7 million were employed, while another 4 million worked on their husband's farms or in their businesses.

PROPAGANDA AND CULTURE

Propaganda was a cornerstone of the Nazi state. By taking control of the radio, Goebbels, the propaganda minister, ensured that Nazi views were broadcast into people's homes, offices and factories every day of the year. The press (nearly 5000 daily newspapers) was not so easy to control, but by channelling news reports through only one news agency, and by daily press briefings for editors at the Propaganda Ministry, a party line on the news was soon established, from which few dared to depart. Film was almost as important as radio for propaganda: without television, cinema was the main visual medium, and most Germans attended the cinema every week, where they would see newsreels and feature films, some of very high quality, that were always officially approved.

German culture was also Nazified. Living artists had to produce work that fitted Nazi ideology regarding Aryan supremacy, nationalism, militarism and so on. Modernist works were regarded as degenerate and were banned. Classical theatre and music tended to flourish, but any works by Jewish composers were banned, and books by Jewish authors were burnt. The German view of the world became what the Nazis wanted Germans to see and hear, and it was invariably pro-Nazi.

OUTSIDERS

The Nazi regime portrayed itself as a 'law-and-order' government, and by using tough methods cracked down on crime, suppressed pornography and swept prostitutes off the streets, gaining much popular support; yet it used the *Gestapo* to spy on its citizens, destroyed legitimate opposition groups and flouted the rules of law itself. This was most clearly seen in its attitude to 'outsiders': those people who did not fit the Nazi mould of the Aryan *Herrenvolk*.

Homosexuals, tramps, gypsies, the physically or mentally handicapped, and the mentally ill – people whose only 'crime' was to be different – were harassed, persecuted and killed. Over 300 000 people were sterilised for being carriers of hereditary illnesses, having schizophrenia or simply being former communists; over 70 000 mentally sick or ill people were gassed under a euthanasia programme; 10 000 tramps or beggars were sent to concentration camps where few survived; and half a million gypsies were murdered when war extended Nazi control over Europe.

The day-to-day reality of life in the Third Reich was that of a police state: a complex mixture of fear, subjugation and bureaucracy for the oppressed, combined with confidence, opportunity and 'freedom' for the fortunate. It all depended upon where you stood or, more importantly, who you were – especially if you happened to be Jewish.

1 How might different sorts of young people have felt about the Hitler Youth?

2 Would young women have reacted differently to the Nazi reforms than older women?

3 What was it like to live in a society surrounded by Nazi propaganda?

Joseph Goebbels, Propaganda Minister

Goebbels had a university education and had gained a doctorate but, unable to find fame or fortune as a writer, had fallen under Hitler's spell and became fanatically loyal to him.

A brilliant propagandist, his wit, intelligence and cynicism made him many enemies both in and outside the party, and he was christened the 'Poison Dwarf' as he was small and walked with a limp. Nevertheless, he had a string of affairs outside his marriage, and fathered five children within it.

One of the 'inner circle', he was made *Gauleiter* of Berlin and then Minister of Propaganda, where he was central in helping to create the 'Hitler myth' of the hard-working, all-caring, omnipotent *Führer*. Out of favour in the early years of the war, he won his influence back by becoming ever more radical and hard-line, demanding more and more sacrifices from the German people to keep the war going at all costs.

Intelligent enough to see the final hopelessness of his position, his last act of 'loyalty' to his *Führer* was to poison his children before committing suicide with his wife.

1 Why was there so much anti-Semitism, and why could the Jews do so little about it?

?

2 Was it possible to be anti-Semitic in general and yet still live with Jewish friends and neighbours?

There is a wide general literature on German, and especially Nazi, attitudes towards the Jews. Try *Life in the Third Reich* by R. Bessel (Oxford University Press, 1987), or *The War against the Jews, 1933–45* by L. S. Dawidowicz (Penguin, 1990).

Try to find out about the two sides of anti-Semitism in Germany. How much of what was done was Official Policy, and how much was Latent Anti-Semitism, albeit greatly encouraged by the Nazis?

Nazi Anti-Semitism: 1933–1939

Hitler and the Nazis did not invent anti-Semitism: hatred of the Jews (as 'murderers' of Jesus Christ, as moneylenders and as convenient scapegoats) had been a European phenomenon for centuries. In the nineteenth century, anti-Semitic parties had actually won seats in the German *Reichstag*, and with many Jews in the professions, business and politics they were an easy target for social resentment. Yet Hitler, an obsessive anti-Semite, was able to raise the latent anti-Semitism felt by many Germans and turn it into an unfeeling hatred, one that was to lead to the near extermination of the Jews in Europe.

THE FIRST STEPS

Nazi policy towards the half million Jews living in Germany was at first hesitant and uncertain. Members of the SA and SS had long been taking unofficial action against individuals, but on 1 April 1933 the first official boycott of Jewish shops was organised. This was not as effective as had been hoped, and was deeply unpopular both in Germany and abroad. The Nazis recognised that overt violence and anti-Semitism were counter-productive (for now), and Hitler was forced to adopt a gradualist approach, restricting his policy to passing laws excluding Jews from the civil service, universities and the professions.

INCREASING PERSECUTION

Once the Nazi dictatorship gained in confidence and power, however, the persecution was restarted and intensified. In the autumn of 1935, the notorious Nuremberg Race Laws were announced: the Reich Citizenship Law deprived Jews of their German citizenship, and marriage (and sexual relations) between Jews and German citizens was forbidden by the Law for the Protection of German Blood. More insidious was the pressure applied to Jews in everyday life. Jewish children at school were humiliated in front of their classes, and school textbooks were rewritten to show Jews as polluters of the Aryan race. Anti-Jewish propaganda streamed from the officially controlled media; and ordinary people began to take their cue from party statements, refusing to serve Jews in shops or hotels and discriminating against them in employment and housing. The Berlin Olympics were a brief respite: anti-Jewish slogans and propaganda vanished from German cities as the Nazi regime put on a respectable face to the world; but afterwards things were as bad as ever. Many Jews now began to emigrate, leaving for countries where their race was not an issue.

KRISTALLNACHT AND AFTER

By 1938, 150 000 Jews had left Germany, yet the pressures on the remainder showed no signs of lifting. Jews were now forced to adopt specifically Jewish forenames – such as 'Israel' or 'Sarah' – and their wealth and property had to be registered. Then, following the assassination of a German diplomat in Paris by a young Jewish activist, the Nazis organised a pogrom of Jews throughout Germany: on *Kristallnacht* thousands of Jewish synagogues, shops and homes were burnt, looted and destroyed; more than 100 Jews were killed; and between 20 000 and 30 000 were imprisoned in concentration camps. This act marked a new stage in the persecution: all Jewish children were now expelled from state schools; all Jewish businesses were forced to close, and were sold; Jews were forced out of all skilled work; public places, such as theatres, parks and beaches, were barred to them; and in April 1939 their remaining wealth was confiscated.

TRAPPED

The 200 000–300 000 Jews left in the German Reich were now trapped. The confiscation of their wealth had left them unable to buy or bribe their way out, and no other country was willing to accept huge numbers of poverty-stricken refugees. The role of the SS in ridding Germany of the Jews was now strengthened, and Hitler began publicly to threaten that war in Europe would mean the 'annihilation of the Jewish race'. On the day that Germany invaded Poland, a curfew for Jews was introduced; and German Jews found themselves an unwanted and hated minority in a country that was about to go to war.

Evidence of official attitudes towards the Jews ...

'Only such measures should be taken which do not involve danger to German life or property. (For instance synagogues are to be burned down only when there is no danger of fire to the surroundings). Business and private apartments of Jews may be destroyed but not looted ... The demonstrations which are going to take place should not be hindered by the police ... As many Jews, especially rich ones, are to be arrested as can be accommodated in the existing prisons ...'

Directions from Heydrich, head of the SD and the Gestapo, sent to state police and SS leaders on Kristallnacht, the night of 9–10 November 1938

... and of the private attitudes of many ordinary Germans

'I had learned from the example of my parents that one could have anti-Semitic opinions without this interfering with one's personal relations with individual Jews ... In preaching that all the misery of the nations was due to the Jews or that the Jewish spirit was seditious and Jewish blood corrupting, I was not compelled to think of ... old Herr Lewy or Rosel Cohn: I thought only of the bogeyman, "The Jew".'

Memoirs of Melita Maschmann

One account of popular anti-Semitism

'Towns and villages put up notices on their approach roads "Jews not wanted here". Holiday resorts advertised themselves as "free of Jewish taint". By 1935 local authorities were banning Jews from public parks and playing fields: it was not unusual to see outside a local swimming pool the notice: "Bathing prohibited to Dogs and Jews".'

Tony Howarth, The World since 1900, 1979

Jews subjected to public humiliation

Kristallnacht – the Night of Broken Glass, referring to the tens of thousands of windows in Jewish homes, synagogues and shops smashed in the attacks of the night of 9–10 November 1938

The Holocaust: 1939–1945

THE KEY ISSUE

Why did the Holocaust happen in Europe between 1939 and 1945?

THE KEY SKILLS

Analysis
Explanation

WHAT YOU HAVE TO DO

Explain why 5 million Jews were killed between 1941 and 1945. Implicit within this is an assessment of the debate between historians.

Were the Jews doomed from the moment Hitler came to power, or did force of circumstance lead to the death camps?

?

Most books on the Third Reich will have at least a chapter on the Holocaust. Many books on the Second World War will also discuss the Nazi 'New Order'. You could also look at G. Fleming's *Hitler and the Final Solution* (University of California Press, 1994) or G. Reitlinger's *The Final Solution* (Jason Aronson, 1987).

As well as the subheadings on these pages, make notes on Hitler's Intentions and The Situation in Europe to find out the 'whys' behind the events.

Einsatzgruppen – 'action squads' of SS troops, set up to eliminate any Jews or communists who they came across, often by mass shootings

Key

Ordnungspolizei – police units sent into occupied areas to 'keep order', which they did by using the same methods as the SS

INTO NAZI HANDS

The conquest and division of Poland put another 2–3 million Jews under the control of the Nazis. For a few months in the winter of 1939–40, Jewish 'reservations' or ghettos were established in occupied Poland, but the war forced a halt to this. With the conquest of western Europe a further half million Jews came under Hitler's power, and for a time it looked as if European Jews might be resettled in the French colony of Madagascar. The continuation of the war made this impossible, but it would not have been an alternative to extermination, as the Nazis seem to have believed that most of the resettled Jews would have died of disease. In the winter of 1940–41, deportations to the Polish ghettos restarted.

WAR OF EXTERMINATION

It was the German invasion of the Soviet Union in June 1941 that was the trigger for the Holocaust, the deliberate extermination of the Jews in Europe. German and Polish Jews had been persecuted, terrorised and deported to ghettos up to now, but few had been deliberately killed. Using the excuse of a 'crusade against Bolshevism', Hitler now ordered a 'war of extermination' against communist officials and Jews. Working behind the German army as it swept into Belarus, the Ukraine and Russia special SS *Einsatzgruppen* units, and armed German police units, the *Ordnungspolizei*, carried out a systematic policy of mass murder. The scale of the killings was unprecedented: by the first week of August 30 000 Jews had been killed by the *Ordnungspolizei* in Belarus; 12 000 Ukrainian Jews were killed in one week alone; and by the spring of 1942 over 1 million Jews had been murdered by the SS, wiping out whole Jewish communities in the Soviet Union.

THE WANNSEE CONFERENCE

The 'success' of this slaughter pointed the way forward. In September 1941 all Jews in German-controlled Europe were forced to wear a yellow Star of David to make them easily recognisable. At the Wannsee Conference in Berlin in January 1942, various agencies concerned with the 'Jewish Problem' agreed on a 'Final Solution': Jews were not to be allowed to emigrate, or to live on in ghettos on more than a temporary basis. Instead, they were to be killed – all of them, and as efficiently as possible.

THE FINAL SOLUTION

The task of implementing the 'Final Solution' was passed to the SS. It had become clear that the mass executions on the Eastern Front were damaging morale and wasting time, and that a more industrial solution was called for. To this end, special extermination camps were constructed in sparsely populated areas of eastern Europe. Gas chambers, crematoria and the other paraphenalia associated with death camps were ordered, tested and built at the ends of railway lines. By the summer of 1943, Auschwitz, Treblinka, Maidanek and the others were ready, and soon the cattle trucks were rolling from all parts of Europe, transporting Jews to their deaths: German Jews, Polish Jews, Jews from Holland, Belgium and France, rich and poor alike, parents, children and grandparents. They were told that they were to be 'resettled'; they were given postcards to send home; then the old, the young and the ill were sent to the 'showers', while the fit and the skilled were set to work sorting through clothes, shoes, spectacles and jewelry, or forced to carry the corpses from the gas chambers to the ovens, or made to extract gold teeth, or shave the hair from the dead. The SS could use nearly everything that the Jews had brought with them: they could sell it through their businesses in the Reich, and make a profit. And once the fit and skilled had been worked to exhaustion, or could not take it any more, they could always be replaced by others.

GENOCIDE

In this way, some 5 million Jews from all over Europe were murdered: whole families and whole communities were wiped out. The key figure is, of course, Adolf Hitler. No documentary evidence exists that links him with the 'Final Solution', but it is inconceivable that he did not order it done, or know about it in detail: as thousands of other Germans must have known of it, and taken part in it – not just those in the SS, but railwaymen, chemists, builders, clerks and others. Many people in Nazi Germany were responsible for this most terrible of crimes.

The debate between historians

- *The 'Intentionalists'*. Hitler was a fanatical anti-Semite who committed himself to the extermination of the Jews from early in his career. All of the policies that he followed from 1933 onwards led inevitably to the 'Final Solution' and the death camps. The Holocaust happened because Hitler wanted it to.

- *The 'Structuralists'*. Until 1939, Hitler was concerned with expulsion rather than extermination. It was the war, the extension of Nazi control over millions more Jews, and the chaotic situation in eastern Europe that forced the improvisation of a policy that led to the Holocaust. The responsibility for the genocide lies with the whole Nazi regime.

The historians' debate

Not all historians agree about everything. In Germany most historians divide into two 'schools' when interpreting and writing about the Nazi period. One school, the 'Intentionalists', believe that Hitler's intentions were clearly set out in *Mein Kampf*, early in his career, and that when he came to power, he and the Nazi Party followed a step-by-step path to fulfilling these plans. Everything in the Nazi period, they argue, was a deliberate move towards Hitler's ultimate goals.

The 'Structuralists', on the other hand, argue that *Mein Kampf* was not a programme but a series of loose ideas, and that when Hitler and the Nazis came to power they proceeded as they did because of circumstance and the situation at the time. Hitler's policies were the result of the political and economic realities that he faced.

The prediction ...

'If the international Jewish financiers in and outside Europe should succeed in plunging the nations into a world war, then the result will be ... the annihilation of the Jewish race in Europe.'

Adolf Hitler, speaking to the Reichstag in January 1939

The outcome ...

The extermination camps

THE KEY ISSUE

To what extent was there a popular opposition to Hitler and the Nazi Party in Germany between 1933 and 1945?

THE KEY SKILLS

Interpretation
Assessment

WHAT YOU HAVE TO DO

Older books on Nazi Germany give little space to this subject. It is only in more recent years that the depth of popular opposition to the Nazis has been realised and begun to be quantified. The nature of the Nazi state made it difficult for open opposition to exist. What you have to assess is whether this opposition was as limited as the few facts that you are likely to find indicate, or whether this was, in fact, merely the tip of an iceberg of discontent that was lying mostly below the surface.

One of the key texts to read here is the section on Youth in Nazi Germany in R. Bessel (ed.) *Life in the Third Reich* (Oxford University Press, 1987). You could also read I. Kershaw's *Popular Opinion and Popular Dissent in the Third Reich: Bavaria 1933–1945* (Clarendon Press, 1984) or any book on German resistance/opposition to Hitler.

Try to distinguish between Individual Opposition and Organised Groups, which themselves could be split further. The headings on these pages concentrate on young people: you could research women, industrial workers or any other group on which you can find information.

The German Opposition 1

There were no elections, or opinion polls, under the Third Reich, so it is impossible to gauge accurately the extent of the support for, or opposition to, Hitler and the Nazi regime. However, it seems reasonable to assume that people who voted for the Communist or socialist parties in the last free and fair elections of the Weimar Republic, in 1932, would be unlikely ever to give their support to a fascist party that was the antithesis of all that they believed in; or that people who had voted consistently for a Catholic Centre Party throughout the 1920s would switch their allegiance to a non-Christian extremist party in the 1930s. It seems likely, then, that at any one time up to 40% of the adult German population were opposed both to the Nazi leadership of their country, and to the policies that they carried out.

INDIVIDUAL PROTESTS

Individuals could make small protests against the regime. By listening to foreign radio broadcasts, reading banned books or telling anti-Nazi jokes, they could assert their independence at small cost to themselves. Artists and intellectuals could criticise the regime obliquely through their work, while others took a more active role, hiding Jews or other enemies of the state. This 'silent opposition' ran risks, for the penalties for these actions could be severe; but although many people did at least some of these things at one time or other, they were largely ineffectual in making any difference at all to the Nazi state.

ORGANISED OPPOSITION

The destruction of independent political parties and trades unions made it difficult for the opposition to establish an organisational base, and the activities of the *Gestapo* meant that the political opposition tended to be in small groups or cells. The SPD was forced to operate from abroad, and had to smuggle its ideas and literature from Prague, and later Paris. The KPD had its lines of communication to Moscow; and the ZP had some backing from Rome; but all opposition groups lacked real assistance from other countries and had to struggle on illegally inside Germany. It says something for their determination that 11 000 people were arrested in 1936 alone for helping the SPD underground in Germany, while between 1933 and 1939 over 112 000 people had been sentenced for political offences.

THE CHURCHES

While the Catholic church had at first come to an accommodation with the Nazis, persecution and interference in church affairs brought a determination by the papacy and Catholic priests to retain as much of their independence as possible. Many thousands of Protestant priests also fought hard against Nazi attempts to absorb the Lutheran church into a new state church, but it is difficult to say whether this was to oppose Hitler or to keep their independence. Most priests appear to have tolerated the Nazi regime, concentrating on giving spiritual comfort to their flocks, but many must have privately held similar views to the 400 or so priests who were executed for openly and persistently criticising Hitler.

YOUNG PEOPLE

Evidence also suggests that opposition to the Nazis was more widespread among young people than has been supposed. Although membership of the Hitler Youth had become compulsory in 1936, by as late as 1939 over 2 million young people remained outside its ranks. Many, undoubtedly, had been kept away from it by their parents; but, equally, many must have made their own decision not to take part in it.

By the war years, youth subcultures openly hostile to the Nazis had appeared: 'Edelweiss Pirates' were groups of working-class teenagers, often apprentices, who rebelled against authority, took unsanctioned weekend trips into the countryside, beat up Hitler Youth patrols and covered subways with anti-Nazi graffiti. On one day in 1942 the *Gestapo* broke up 28 of these gangs containing over 700 teenagers, and by 1944 these youth gangs were becoming such a problem that a dozen of their leaders were publicly hanged. At the other end of the spectrum was the 'Swing' movement: upper-middle-class youths with money, clothes and status, who would dance to American swing and jazz music, wear English-style clothes, and take pleasure in a sexuality that the authorities would call 'degenerate'. Most young people would not have followed either of these trends, but enough did to cause the authorities genuine concern.

Two 'swing types', from an official book on youth criminality, 1941

Disaffected youth

Just how concerned the authorities were by the growth of a youth 'counter-culture' in Germany during the Second World War may be seen by this report by the Dusseldorf branch of the Nazi Party to the *Gestapo* on 17 July 1943:

'Re. "Edelweiss Pirates". The said youths are throwing their weight around again. I have been told that gatherings of young people have become more conspicuous than ever [in a local park] especially since the last air-raid on Dusseldorf. These adolescents, aged between 12 and 17, hang around into the late evening with musical instruments and young females. Since this riff-raff is in large part outside the Hitler Youth and adopts a hostile attitude towards the organisation, they represent a danger to other young people. It has recently been established that members of the armed forces too are to be found among these young people and they, owing to their membership in the [army] exhibit particularly arrogant behaviour. There is a suspicion that it is these youths who have covered the walls of the pedestrian subway on the Altenbergstrasse with the slogans 'Down with Hitler', 'The OKW [Military High Command] is lying', 'Medals for Murder', 'Down with Nazi Brutality' etc. However often these inscriptions are removed, within a few days new ones reappear on the walls.'

Reports like this one, and the photographs here, rather dent the myth that all young Germans during the Nazi era were uniformed, well-disciplined members of the Hitler Youth.

THE KEY ISSUE

To what extent was there organised opposition in the German army to Hitler between 1933 and 1945?

THE KEY SKILLS

Interpretation
Assessment

WHAT YOU HAVE TO DO

What you have to consider here is much the same as you considered earlier in this chapter. How much opposition was there in the army to Hitler, and were the plots to kill him the result of just a few discontented officers, or the visible expression of a hidden and much deeper malaise inside the German army?

As well as the books already mentioned, you could look at *The Reichswehr and Politics* by F. L. Carsten (University of California Press, 1973); or *Army, Politics and Society in Germany* by K. J. Müller (Manchester University Press, 1987).

This section concentrates on the German Army, because it was chiefly the only organisation in Nazi Germany with the power to overthrow Hitler. However, important headings are also The Morale of the People and The Terroristic State when trying to explain why no major popular attempt was made to unseat Hitler and establish another form of government.

The German Opposition 2

CIVILIAN MORALE

Only two things could force the overthrow of the Nazis from within Germany: a popular uprising, or a *coup d'état* by the army. The first could only have come about spontaneously as a result of a disastrous breakdown in living standards, as had happened at the end of the first World War some 20 years earlier, and to counteract this the Nazi leadership made certain that civilian morale was always given a very high priority. For example, near the beginning of the war workers' bonuses and wage rates were hastily restored after having been cut; and up until 1944 rations were always adequate, and above the minimum necessary for existence. Moreover, when there was genuine popular hostility to a policy that was not absolutely central to Nazi beliefs: for example, the gassing of 70 000 mentally and physically handicapped Germans between 1939 and 1941, it was quickly stopped on Hitler's orders.

THE ARMY

An overthrow of the government by the army was also unlikely. The standard of professionalism in the German army was very high, as were its traditions of loyalty and obedience. To have broken their oath to serve the *Führer* was something that most German soldiers would simply not have considered. Nevertheless, there were enough high-ranking officers who considered that their first duty was to Germany, and not Hitler, to make a coup a possibility. Certainly, by 1938, many generals were unhappy about the direction in which German foreign policy was going: Hitler's march into the Rhineland was against their advice, they had been humiliated over the sacking of their Commander-in-Chief and his replacement by Hitler, and they feared being dragged into a general European war over the Sudetenland. Plans were actually drawn up to arrest Hitler and declare martial law once the fighting had started; but the Munich settlement scuppered all this, and from then on Hitler's run of victories kept the generals quiet.

THE ESTABLISHMENT

Yet there were many leading members of the German establishment who continued secretly to oppose Hitler, and who maintained contacts with the army: aristocrats, ambassadors, civil servants, intellectuals – individuals who met informally, who exchanged ideas, and who gradually formed anti-Nazi groups, such as the Kreisau Circle. Such people lived in constant fear of infiltrators and informers, and had their difficulties made worse by the Allies' demands for 'unconditional surrender', which encouraged many Germans to fight on who otherwise might not have done so. Yet by 1943 it was clear that the only way to save Germany from disaster was to get rid of Hitler, declare martial law and set up a new government.

THE JULY BOMB PLOT

An assassination attempt was organised: on 20 July 1944 a Colonel von Stauffenberg placed a bomb under a table next to where Hitler was sitting while he was holding a meeting at his 'Wolf's Lair' H.Q. in East Prussia. The bomb exploded, but only after it had been casually kicked to the other side of a massive oak table support, which took much of the blast. Hitler was hurt, but not fatally, and the conspirators in Berlin had refused to act until they knew he was dead. Their delay destroyed the plot: the SS were able to arrest and torture suspects, and 5000 opposition figures were rounded up and executed.

ILLUSION AND REALITY

Although Nazi propaganda liked to portray Germany under Hitler as a united nation, marching forward in step together under one leader, the reality was very different. There was an extensive opposition to the Nazis all the way through the time of the Third Reich. Millions of Germans were secretly critical of all that the Nazis stood for; and tens of thousands actively opposed the regime; but, like people everywhere when faced with the threat of imprisonment or death for speaking out against a violent and terroristic state, most kept silent for the sake of themselves and their families, hoping to survive until better times; and so, paradoxically, helped to create the illusion of unity that gave the Nazi state the strength to survive.

Plots to kill Hitler

Although many people, such as intellectuals, communists and army officers, had discussed getting rid of Hitler for many years, it was only from 1943, when the war seemed to be lost, that any serious attempts were made to kill Hitler; and there were a number besides the July Bomb plot, outlined on these pages.

Because, at this time, Hitler was out of reach, directing the war from his East Prussian headquarters, the only people capable of killing him were army officers, and a surprising number were willing to do it. The most sure way, without losing one's own life, was to place a bomb near to the *Führer* and not be there when it went off, as von Stauffenberg tried to do, and as two other anti-Nazi officers did, when they smuggled a bomb aboard Hitler's plane: however, the bomb failed to explode.

Some German officers were, however, willing to die themselves ...

'The next day I carried in each of my overcoat pockets a bomb with a 10-minute fuse. I intended to stay as close to Hitler as I could, so that he at least would be blown to pieces by the explosion. When Hitler ... entered the exhibition hall, Schmundt came across to me and said that only 8–10 minutes were to be spent on inspecting the exhibits. So the possibility of carrying out the assassination no longer existed, since ... the fuse needed at least 10 minutes.'

Colonel Gersdorff, German army

At least three further 'overcoat' attempts on Hitler's life were made, but all were frustrated.

THE KEY ISSUES

- How was Hitler able to re-establish Germany as a great power by 1936?
- Did Hitler intentionally follow a policy towards world power?

THE KEY SKILLS

Interpretation
Assessment

WHAT YOU HAVE TO DO

Use the two Key Issues as questions. Remember: what we're really interested in here is not so much what happened – although that is important – as why it happened.

Was German foreign policy all the result of Hitler's master plan, or were there other forces at work?

Because there are many different interpretations of Hitler's foreign policy, there are many different books on the subject. For a balanced view, see I. Kershaw's *Hitler* (Longman, 1991) or W. Carr's *Arms, Autarky and Aggression* (Edward Arnold, 1979). For a different view, see D. Irving's *Hitler's War* (Focal Point, 1991).

A warning: this is not an easy topic. There is a great deal of debate over Hitler's aims, and many twists and turns to follow. What you have to do is clearly establish The Pattern of Events, and then assess which events were important in re-establishing Germany as a Great Power.

German Foreign Policy 1933–1936

GERMAN AND NAZI FOREIGN POLICY AIMS

Although the foreign policy followed by Germany in the years after 1933 had its roots in an earlier era – it was Bismarck who had formed the German Empire, while the overturning of the Treaty of Versailles was the ultimate aim of many Weimar politicians – it was the Nazi Party, and especially Hitler, who gave it its particular slant. The bringing of all the German *Volk* into one greater German *Reich*, and the need for *Lebensraum* in the east to accommodate the expanding *Volk*, were specifically Nazi policies, and were the inevitable consequence to Germany regaining great power status. There is little doubt that Hitler had this ultimate aim in mind in all his dealings with the other European powers:

'We put an end to the perpetual Germanic march towards the south and west of Europe and turn our eyes towards the lands of the east. We finally put a stop to the colonial and commercial policy of pre-war times and pass over to the territorial policy of the future. But when we speak of new territory in Europe today, we must principally think of Russia and the border states subject to her... This colossal empire in the east is ripe for dissolution.'

Adolf Hitler, Mein Kampf, 1924

THE WEAKENING OF THE VERSAILLES SETTLEMENT

Hitler came to power at a time when the Versailles settlement was already breaking down. France and Britain had evacuated the Rhineland, and reparations payments had been cancelled. American isolationism was at its height, and the rise of Japan in the Far East was worrying Britain. There was a strong feeling in many European capitals that Germany had been badly treated in 1919, a feeling that the Nazis were keen to play up. So when, in 1933, Germany walked out of the Disarmament Conference and the League of Nations, feelings in Europe were more of sorrow than fear or anger, especially as Hitler preached peace.

EARLY MOVES

To pursue his aims, Hitler needed to weaken France and cultivate Britain or Italy. A bi-lateral pact with Poland broke up the French alliance system in eastern Europe; but Hitler's support for the attempted coup by the Austrian Nazis in 1934 frightened Mussolini so much that he moved troops to the Austrian border, and his announcement of the existence of the *Luftwaffe*, and the reintroduction of conscription in 1935 (breaking the Versailles Treaty) brought Italy, Britain and France together in the Stresa Front. It seemed as if Hitler was getting nowhere, and yet within a few months the situation was transformed.

THE GROWTH OF GERMAN INFLUENCE

The Anglo-German Naval Agreement of 1935 was seen by Britain as a chance to limit an expanding German navy; yet it was another nail in the coffin of Versailles, and it broke up the Stresa Front. France and Britain were then forced to condemn the Italian invasion of Abyssinia, while doing next to nothing about it, showing the weakness of the League of Nations and driving Italy into Germany's arms. The Saarland had already voted to return to Germany in a plebiscite, and Hitler was now able to take advantage of the confusion of the other European powers by marching German troops into the demilitarised Rhineland in March 1936. This was a bold gamble and a major coup for Hitler: it was a flagrant breach of what was left of Versailles; it removed the buffer zone between France and Germany; and it was a domestic triumph for Hitler. The French did nothing to stop it, and a common British attitude was that Hitler was only marching into his own backyard. German and Italian intervention in the Spanish Civil War later that year – contrary to strenuous British and French non-intervention – only served to emphasise the close political, military and ideological ties between Hitler and Mussolini, culminating in the Rome–Berlin Axis of November.

THE END OF THE FIRST PHASE

By the end of 1936 there was little doubt that Hitler had achieved a succession of striking foreign policy successes. By taking bold initiatives and refusing to be bound by normal diplomatic procedure; because of French and British reluctance to act against him; and through British and Italian willingness to sacrifice international co-operation for their own benefit, Hitler had been able to tear up the Treaty of Versailles, re-establish Germany as a great power, and fill a power vacuum in the heart of Europe. With these pre-conditions established, Hitler was now able to move on to the next phase of his foreign policy intentions.

The debate between historians

- The *'Intentionalists'*. Hitler had a clear set of foreign policy objectives – supremacy in Europe followed by world power status – and he followed a stage-by-stage programme towards these ends. His character and ideas were central to the creation of a specifically Nazi foreign policy in these years, based on race and the theories of Lebensraum.
- The *'Structuralists'*. German foreign policy was a reflection of Hitler's ideas of expansionism, but external and internal pressures determined the pace of events. The various Nazi foreign 'bureaux', the dynamism of the Nazi movement, domestic economic pressures, and the reactions of Britain and France all shaped Nazi foreign policy and forced Hitler to adapt to events.

Remember the historians' debate? Read these sources and decide whether the 'Intentionalists' or the 'Structuralists' have the right answer.

Why was the Italian invasion of Abyssinia important for Hitler?

'Either Mussolini will stumble and get himself so heavily involved in Africa that he will be greatly weakened in Europe, whereupon Hitler can seize Austria, hitherto protected by the Duce; or he will win, defying France and Britain, and thereupon be ripe for a tie-up with Hitler against the Western democracies. Either way Hitler wins.'

William L. Shirer, Berlin Diary, 1941

Why was the March into the Rhineland such a bold step for Hitler?

'The 48 hours after the march into the Rhineland were the most nerve-racking of my life. If the French had then marched into the Rhineland we would have had to withdraw with our tail between our legs, for the military resources at our disposal would have been wholly inadequate for even a modest resistance.'

Adolf Hitler

'Considering the situation we were in, the French covering army could have blown us to pieces.'

Alfred Jodl, German general

So why didn't the French act? The French government wanted to but ...

'General Gamelin [French CGS] advised that a war operation, however limited, entailed unpredictable risks and could not be undertaken without decreeing a general mobilisation.'

François-Poncet, French ambassador to Germany, 1936

THE KEY ISSUE

Why did Nazi foreign policy lead to war in 1939?

THE KEY SKILLS

Interpretation
Explanation

WHAT YOU HAVE TO DO

Try to explain the steps that Hitler took in his foreign policy from 1937. Try to answer the Key Issue. A lot depends upon what you believe Hitler's aims were. Given all that you have read, do you think that the assessment here is correct – or is there another explanation?

Apart from the books that you have already studied, you could look at A. J. P. Taylor's *Origins of the Second World War* (Penguin, 1985), which considers Nazi foreign policy from the point of view of old-fashioned great power politics.

Use the subheadings on these pages: to understand Nazi foreign policy, a step-by-step approach to the sequence of events on the road to war is helpful.

1 Did Hitler want a war with Britain and France?
2 Why did Britain and France go to war over Poland?

The Road to War: 1937–1939

By the end of 1937, Germany was in a much stronger position. Rearmament was well under way, and the Four Year Plan had been established to place the economy on a war footing; Italy had joined Germany and Japan in the Anti-Comintern Pact, establishing a grouping which seemed to threaten Britain and France in both Europe and East Asia; Versailles was dead, if not yet buried, and Germany was the dominant power on the continent. Hitler could now confidently demand much more in Europe, and could back up these demands with the threat of armed force, or military power itself, to secure his aims.

Anschluss with Austria

The Austrian Nazi movement had re-established itself since 1934, and was now undermining the country. With Mussolini content to let events take their course, and with Britain and France unconcerned, Hitler put pressure on the Austrian government to yield to internal and external pressure and allow an *Anschluss*. To forestall a referendum on the issue, and with an 'invitation' from Austrian Nazis to do so, Hitler invaded in March 1938 and, meeting a tumultuous reception, absorbed Austria into the German Reich.

The Destruction of Czechoslovakia

The Sudeten Germans provided the excuse for Hitler's next move in Europe. Czechoslovakia, a creation of Versailles, had been one of the few successful democracies in eastern Europe, but had also always been an uneasy mix of half a dozen nationalities. With the Nazi Sudeten German Party stirring up grievances among the German minority, Hitler prepared to smash the Czech state; but the Czechs proved more robust in the defence of their country than the Austrians, and prepared to fight. Britain and France, desperate to keep the peace in Europe, made it clear they would not tolerate a German invasion; but in the face of repeated pressure from Hitler decided that a peaceful solution to the Czech 'problem' was acceptable. At the Munich Conference in September 1938, appeasement triumphed and the Czech state was dismembered: the Sudetenland, with all of its economic and military assets, was given to Germany, and 3 million more Germans joined the Reich. Shortly afterwards, Poland seized Teschen, and the Hungarians took southern Slovakia.

Six months later, Hitler used the separatist demands of the Slovaks and the territorial demands of the Hungarians to provoke the break-up of the country. Germany annexed Bohemia and Moravia as a 'Protectorate', a Slovak puppet state was set up and Hungary moved into Ruthenia. The Czech state ceased to exist as a separate country and the German Reich now dominated central Europe.

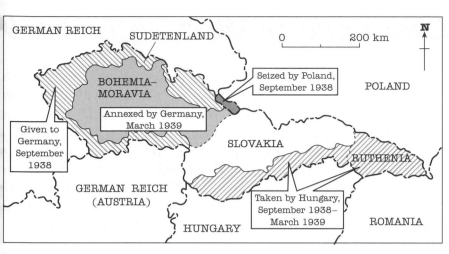

The destruction of Czechoslovakia

POLAND

Two weeks after the annexation, Britain and France guaranteed the security of Poland. It had now become obvious to the Western powers that Hitler's ambitions in Europe were too great to be stopped by diplomacy, and that only the threat of war would do. Yet Hitler was not contemplating war with Britain and France, at least not in the short term. He was going to fight in Poland, partly to reclaim territories lost at Versailles, and partly for *Lebensraum*; but he hoped to expand here without Western intervention. The Pact of Steel with Italy was one way of preventing this, for it sealed a military alliance across central Europe which the Western powers could not cross. The Nazi–Soviet Non-Aggression Pact of August 1939 was another, for as well as delivering Soviet acquiescence in the invasion of Poland, it deprived Britain and France of their only possible ally in preventing this. Hitler was convinced that neither Britain nor France would now stand by their guarantees, and proceeded to launch the invasion on 1 September. When, two days later, they did declare war on Germany, Hitler found himself in a major conflict that he did not want.

HITLER'S ULTIMATE AIMS?

It may be that, in time, Hitler's Germany would have felt ready to launch a large-scale war against Britain and France, in order to determine which would be a leading world, rather than a European, power. The thrust of German foreign policy suggests, however, that Hitler was planning for Poland to be just another small-scale localised conflict, one more step along the road to the major war that Hitler was always expecting to fight: in the east, against Soviet Russia, not in the west against Britain and France. By defeating the Soviet Union, Hitler would have gained most of what he had always wanted: *Lebensraum*, the destruction of communism, and the establishment of a German *Herrenvolk* in Europe.

THE KEY ISSUES

- Why were German forces fighting across Europe and in North Africa between 1939 and 1945?
- To what extent was the German economy on a war footing between 1939 and 1945?

THE KEY SKILLS

Assessment
Analysis

WHAT YOU HAVE TO DO

Analyse the course of the war. Explain the different reasons – military, political and ideological – for German troops fighting in and occupying Scandinavia, western Europe, North Africa, the Balkans and Russia.

To what extent was the German economy geared up for war between 1939 and 1945? **?**

This chapter is not about the Second World War: it is about the part that the German state and people played in that war, and how the war affected them.

There are many books, films and videos about the 'Second World War'. Look at M. Gilbert's book *Second World War* (Phoenix Giants, 1995); *Total War* by P. Calvocoressi (Penguin, 1995); or Thames TV's *The World at War* for the part that Germany played. For The *German Economy at War*, see A. Milward's book (Athlone Press, 1965) or, for an inside account, read A. Speer's *Inside the Third Reich* (Phoenix, 1995).

Germany at War: 1939–1945

BLITZKRIEG

Using *Blitzkrieg* techniques, the German army was able to overrun Poland in three weeks, after which the country was divided between Germany and the USSR. Hitler now made concerted efforts to end the state of war with Britain and France which the invasion had triggered, but was unable to. With his patience exhausted, and wishing to secure his western flank, Hitler ordered the over-running of western Europe in the spring of 1940. Once again, the *Blitzkrieg* succeeded, and the war was over in ten weeks. Hitler had destroyed France; but was unable to make peace with, or invade and conquer, Britain. Moreover, before the German army was able to invade the Soviet Union, Hitler had to send German troops to North Africa to help Italian forces there, and launch further *Blitzkrieg* attacks against Yugoslavia and Greece to secure his southeastern flank – and, once again, help out his Italian ally.

OPERATION BARBAROSSA

On 22 June 1941 the German army launched a massive attack against the Soviet Union. It was the culmination of all of Hitler's policies and, like all his other military actions, it was designed to be a *Blitzkrieg*, over in a matter of weeks. At first the German army did achieve stunning victories, capturing city after city and hundreds of thousands of prisoners; but unlike western Europe the vast distances of Russia, the heroic resistance of the Soviet forces and the weather combined to halt the German advance short of its objectives. The war in the east now became a slow and terrible agony for the German army, bleeding it to death. When Hitler declared war on the USA, following the Japanese attack on Pearl Harbor, he committed his armed forces to a war they could not possibly win.

WAR IN THE WESTERN HEMISPHERE

By his policies, Hitler had over-extended his forces. Had Britain and France conceded to Hitler over Poland in 1939, the whole weight of the German war machine could have been turned against Russia in the spring of 1940. As it was, German forces found themselves fighting in Scandinavia, western Europe, the north Atlantic, North Africa, the Balkans and later Italy, as well as being tied down as occupying forces in these areas for years on end. Without this fatal dispersal of his forces, Hitler's war against Russia could have been won.

THE GERMAN ECONOMY TO 1941

The other problem that Hitler failed properly to address was the German economy. The German armed forces had been designed for *Blitzkrieg*, and not only carried out this job, but also adapted themselves remarkably well to the task of total war. However, while the German economy had been mobilised towards the demands of a limited war from 1936 under Göring's Four Year Plan (for example, of all German investment, two-thirds had been directed towards war-related projects), by 1940 only a little over one-third of Germany's GNP was going on military expenditure, while in Britain it was well over one-half. The effect of this was the semblance of a peacetime economy in Germany well into 1941.

THE GERMAN ECONOMY AT WAR

It was only after the failure of Barbarossa in the winter of 1941–1942 that the German economy began to shift on to a true war footing. Speer, the new Minister for Armaments, implemented a better organisation for the munitions and equipment industries, adopting mass production techniques, and allocating raw materials where they were needed. At the same time, Sauckel was given control of labour, and used women, conscripted foreign workers and put Russian slave labour to work. The effect of this was to boost the production of armaments right through 1943 and 1944, in spite of Allied bombing. However, with the *Gauleiter* local officials competing with the Reich government, and each other, all through the war for labour and raw materials to keep the industries in their own areas functioning, and with the SS having their own economic empire to control and supply, the German economy could never be as efficient as the Allied ones, and it is surprising that it functioned as well as it did for so long.

Remember: you do not need to know what German forces were doing in the war (except as background). You need to know *why* they were there. Headings could therefore be given for every theatre of war.

The percentage of GNP spent on military expenditure by countries: 1939–1945

	Germany	USA	Britain
1939	23	1	22
1940	38	2	53
1941	47	11	60
1942	55	31	64
1943	61	42	63
1944	*	42	62
1945	*	36	53

*German figures for 1944–1945 are incomplete or not known.

Blitzkrieg – 'lightning war': a sudden, overwhelming attack upon an enemy by planes, tanks and motorised infantry acting together, usually focusing on key points in an enemy's defences and exploiting weaknesses once behind enemy lines

GNP – Gross National Product, the value of all of the goods and services produced by a country

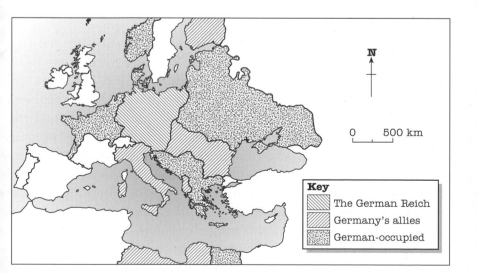

Key
- The German Reich
- Germany's allies
- German-occupied

Germany's expansion into Europe and North Africa, 1942

THE KEY ISSUE

To what extent did the Second World War affect the German people?

THE KEY SKILLS

Analysis
Assessment

WHAT YOU HAVE TO DO

Analyse a broad range of civilian and military factors to assess the condition of the German people between 1939 and 1945, and to what extent this changed over time.

In addition to general books on the Third Reich, you could look at *The Ordeal of Total War, 1939–1945* by G. Wright (Harper & Row, 1968); *The SS: Alibi of a Nation 1922–1945* by G. Reitlinger (Arms and Armour, 1981); *Inside the Third Reich* by A. Speer (Phoenix, 1995); and *The Last Days of Hitler* by H. Trevor-Roper (Macmillan, 1995).

You need to look at the expansion of The Nazi Party and the SS in these years; how the mood of the people changed over time; the effects of Allied Bombing; the Military Defeats; and what life was like for the people in The Last Year of the war.

Inside the Reich: 1939–1945

THE PARTY AND THE PEOPLE

As in other countries, the war provided the opportunity for the state to increase its powers – and in Germany this included the Nazi Party and the SS. The party intensified propaganda efforts to sustain the morale of the people, renewed attacks on the churches, and gained greater powers at local level when the *Gauleiter* officials were appointed Reich Defence Commissioners, with ultimate control over all civil authorities in their area. The party also tightened its grip on the civil service and the appointment of teachers, and began to influence judges over their verdicts. Even the *Volkssturm*, a home guard set up in the last year of the war, was more of a party militia than a military organisation.

THE SS STATE

The SS continued to develop as a 'state within a state'. The *Gestapo* and SD now operated at will, spying on any real or imagined enemies of the state. The SS itself was given the job of military intelligence in 1944, and by the last two years of the war the *Waffen* SS had expanded to a nominal 35 divisions. The SS continued to guard the concentration and extermination camps, and made huge profits from the work and resources of the people incarcerated there. A huge network of firms was controlled by the SS, making everything from armaments to mineral water. By 1945 Himmler's power was second only to that of the *Führer*.

HOPE AND FEAR

Life for the German people did not dramatically change for the first two years of the war. Strict food rationing was brought in from 1939, and because of the Allied blockade *ersatz* products replaced many real ones; but the military successes of 1939–1941, especially the victories of April–June 1940, buoyed up the population, and postponed the need to put civilians under the strain of total war. The Russian campaign, however, marked a fundamental change in the mood of the population. Its failure, in the winter snows outside Moscow, and Hitler's declaration of war on the USA a week later, altered the perception of the German people: a series of short, successful campaigns now had to become a long war of attrition, a war in which the German people themselves would be in the front line.

ersatz – products made from substitutes, e.g. coffee from acorns

THE CONSEQUENCES OF WAR

From 1942, the full consequences of total war began to be felt in Germany. The increasing need for armaments brought more and more men, and women, into the factories, where they found themselves working longer hours for decreasing rewards. As victories gave way to defeats, such as El Alamein and Stalingrad, the morale of the people faltered; although thanks to the propaganda of Goebbels, and an apparently unshakeable belief by the people in Hitler, it never completely collapsed. However, the bombing of the RAF had perhaps the greatest single physical impact on the people: its 'area bombing' techniques (developed only because it lacked the skill to bomb precisely) targeted whole cities, deliberately destroying houses, schools and hospitals as well as factories, docks and railways. This policy not only killed hundreds of thousands of civilians, as at Hamburg and Dresden, but also wiped out much of the country's infrastructure, leaving many of its cities as blackened shells.

The effects of Allied bombing on Germany

'Many German cities presented partial areas of vast devastation. Perhaps the outstanding example was Hamburg, where a series of attacks in July and August of 1943 destroyed 55 to 60% of the city, did damage to an area of 30 square miles; completely burned out 12.5 square miles, wiped out 300,000 homes and made 75,000 people homeless. German estimates range from 60–100,000 killed.'

Taken from the US Strategic Bombing Survey, 1945

THE END OF THE THIRD REICH

The last year of the war brought catastrophe to Germany. Shortages of food, coal and other raw materials led to a cold and hungry population surviving – in many cities at least – in cellars at night, emerging to work in shattered factories by day. Almost everyone had now lost a husband, brother or son in the fighting, and influxes of refugees, mainly fleeing from the advancing Russians in the east, added to the chronic social and economic difficulties. When Silesia and the Ruhr were occupied by the Allies, what was left of the German economy virtually ceased to function. Hitler, returning to Berlin from East Prussia, where he had spent much of the war, was by this time a shadow of his former self, and yet still commanded the absolute loyalty of his henchmen. Only at the very last, when he was alone in his bunker and apparently determined to leave Germany a wasteland, did his colleagues desert him, either to save themselves, or to save something of their country. When Hitler shot himself, on 30 April 1945, his 'Thousand-Year Reich' collapsed in just one week.

After the war was over ...

'One train, which arrived in Berlin on August 31st [1945], started from Danzig [Poland] on the 24th with 325 patients and orphans from the Marien Hospital and Orphanage ... They were packed into 5 cattle trucks, with nothing to cover the floors, not even straw. There were no doctors, nurses or medical supplies ... Between six and ten of the patients in each truck died during the journey. The bodies were simply thrown out of the train...'

Report from the Manchester Guardian, 1945

EPILOGUE

The sufferings of the German people in Europe did not end in 1945. In the two years after the end of the war, some 16 million Germans were expelled from Poland, the Sudetenland, Hungary and other countries in eastern Europe where their ancestors had lived for centuries. They may or may not have been Nazis: it was enough that they were German, and some 2 million of them died on their journey 'home'. They returned to an occupied country, split into four zones, where industrial plant was carried off as reparations by the occupying powers, where starving children scoured rubbish dumps looking for food, and where mothers sold themselves to soldiers in exchange for cigarettes. Such was the destiny of the German people under Adolf Hitler.

The consequences of bombing

Hamburg after an Allied bombing raid

A synthesis is a combining together of different concepts to make a complex whole. This chapter attempts to tie together all of the things covered so far, to give you some answers to the questions you have been posing.

The five questions posed at the start of the book are the key issues in this topic and this chapter tries to answer them here.

Hence this section reflects the three stages of the A-level process: the author has considered the questions posed all through the book; he has weighed the evidence found; and has come to the conclusions presented here.

This is what a synthesis should be: not just the acquisition of a body of knowledge, but a critical understanding of the concepts and issues underlying that knowledge. If you can synthesise this topic then you can be sure that you really understand it.

What if you don't agree with someone else's synthesis?

If you have studied most of this topic so far, you will know that there are many different questions that you can ask relating to Nazi Germany. There are very many pieces of evidence that you can consider; and there are many different interpretations that you will come across – remember, for example, the debate between the 'Intentionalists' and the 'Structuralists'.

Everyone who studies this topic will have their own view of it. If the author had interests in a different area, the book would be a different book and slanted in a particular direction. It would have asked other questions and considered different pieces of evidence, and may well have come to a different synthesis.

Synthesis

1. Why did the Weimar Republic Fail?

Proclaimed amidst the chaos that was Germany in 1918, the new Republic seemed like the least worst option to a nation struggling with the political, social and economic consequences of a lost war. But it was never truly popular: armed groups of both the extreme left and right tried to destroy it; it lost credibility when it signed a peace treaty most Germans regarded as unfair; and, by allowing strict proportional representation and an elected President with special powers, its constitution ensured weak government and a future tyranny.

That the Weimar Republic remained in place was due to democracy being (just) firmly enough established in Germany for the centre parties to work together to ensure its survival, in spite of the political alienation of right and left, and the terrible economic disaster of hyperinflation. It was also helped by the arrival of loans from America, which propped up its ailing economy, and gave the illusion of prosperity in the late 1920s, even though at least one-third of the country failed to share in this.

When the Great Depression arrived from America in the 1930s the fragility of German 'prosperity' was exposed. The withdrawal of the loans that underpinned the German economy led to the widespread closure of factories, bank failures, poverty and ruin for the middle classes, and mass unemployment for the industrial workers. Politicians, who had been unable to co-operate for very long in normal times, were totally unable to work together to solve this emergency, and fell back on relying on the emergency powers of the President to keep the country going. This played into the hands of the extremists. The people lost faith in conventional politicians and turned to the extreme right or left, who appeared to offer easy solutions to complex problems. Once the politicians who believed in democracy lost the trust of the people, the Weimar Republic was doomed.

Yet it could have survived. In 1928 the Republic appeared to be stable and prosperous: it was the economic blizzard of the Depression that destroyed democracy in Germany, and was to blame for the collapse of the Weimar Republic. Throughout the rest of Europe the story was the same: governments crumbled under the strain of economic collapse in a phenomenon that was world-wide.

2. Why did Hitler and the Nazis, and not some other Political Force, Come to Power in 1933?

The NSDAP, or Nazi Party, was the creation of one man: Adolf Hitler. A brilliant speaker and propagandist, he transformed an unknown discussion group into a military-style organisation with himself as its leader. This claimed to be both nationalist and socialist, but was, in essence, fascist in outlook. Unlike Mussolini in Italy, however, he failed to bully his way into government, and instead determined to come to power legally, while following a racist, expansionist programme that only appealed to those on the far right. This combination of factors led to the marginalisation of the party, and by 1929 the Nazis had less than 3% of the vote and seemed to be heading for oblivion.

The Great Depression both saved and made Hitler. With the democratic politicians of the Weimar Republic unable to stop the effects of the slump, the Nazi Party, with its strong organisation, tireless leader and sophisticated propaganda, now came into its own. By promising simple solutions to complex problems, and by careful targeting of key sections of German society – peasant farmers, craftsmen, women, young people – the Nazi vote rose to 18% in the 1930 elections, and the party was established as a serious political force. After that, as the slump deepened, so support for the party rose, until in 1932 it had over one-third of the vote and was the largest single party in Parliament.

However, more than half of the population never voted for the Nazi Party: liberals, Catholics and industrial workers continued to elect democratic or left-wing politicians. Yet these were never able to form a credible parliamentary alternative by working together, because of their own petty differences or ideological splits.

Even if they had put their differences on one side, they would not have come to power. By this time real influence in the land lay with the conservative elites surrounding the President: aristocrats, landowners and army officers, people who had never had much sympathy for Weimar democracy, and who would never have invited a coalition containing, say, the Communists, to form a government. Since 1930 these people had been making and breaking governments, ruling by presidential decree, and in 1933 they intended to continue to do so, inviting Hitler and the Nazis in as junior partners in a nationalist–Nazi coalition, which they fully intended to control. In fact it was Hitler, the ruthless politician, who seized the chance offered to him, and used the mechanisms that he had inherited to overthrow the last vestiges of the Weimar system, and impose Nazi rule upon Germany.

Over the page there are two further pieces of writing about Nazi Germany. Both are conclusions to famous books about the Nazi era, one written by a journalist, and the other by an eminent historian. They act as syntheses in their own way. Compare them and see what you think of them.

3. Did the Nazis Achieve a 'Social Revolution' in Germany?

The Nazis were determined to achieve social as well as economic change in Germany, and underpinned this by a political revolution when Parliament was persuaded to give Hitler dictatorial powers, the trades unions and state governments were brought under Nazi control, and other political parties were abolished. By eliminating the threat from the SA, and taking over the office of President, Hitler was able to become supreme leader, or *Führer*, of Germany, and place his followers into positions of power in the fields of economics, culture, youth, the police and the security services.

By a combination of state investment and rearmament, the Nazis turned around the German economy and claimed to have improved conditions for industrial workers, the peasantry and the middle classes. By putting their ideology to work in the classroom, among women, by clever use of propaganda and by targeting 'outsiders' as well as legitimate opposition groups, the Nazis could portray a united Germany striding forward with one purpose.

The reality was different. Ordinary people made individual protests against the Nazi state; organised opposition lived on underground; churches became a centre for resistance; young people (as they always will!) rebelled against the establishment. Full employment, and Hitler's foreign policy successes, kept most people quiet, but as *Blitzkrieg* turned to attrition, and the casualty lists lengthened in the Second World War, the morale of the German people faltered, and the increasing interference of the Nazi Party and the SS in everyday life was necessary to bolster the Nazis' waning hold on the people. The plots to kill Hitler illustrate the bankruptcy of the Nazi 'social revolution' by 1945.

4. Why was there a Genocide in Europe between 1939 and 1945?

There is a long history of anti-Semitism in Europe, stretching back to the Middle Ages. The young Hitler had absorbed this, along with rabid nationalism and a misunderstood social Darwinism, as he drifted about the streets of Vienna before the First World War.

He developed this into his own view of the world, in which race and nation were the keys, natural selection would weed out the weak, those without a nation were to be despised, and only those deemed worthy were to be allowed to join the *Volk*. On coming to power these ideas began to be put into practice: the idea of the master race was promoted; Jews were increasingly persecuted and 'persuaded' to leave Germany; and those who did not fit the Aryan stereotype were forced into concentration camps, or quietly killed in the name of science.

The first two years of the Second World War brought millions more

European Jews under Nazi control, and the continuation of the war made the expulsion of these Jews from Europe impossible. It was one of the key tenets of Nazi ideology that a German 'master race' could only dominate Europe if the continent was free of Jewish 'taint'. How was this now to be achieved?

The mass killings of Jews and communists in the wake of the German invasion of Russia showed the Nazis a way out of their dilemma. A 'Final Solution' to the Jewish problem could be attempted and hidden under the fog of war. Extermination camps were constructed in remote areas of eastern Europe, and millions of Jews were routinely transported to their deaths. This happened because of the will of the Nazi leadership, but also because of the terroristic nature of the Nazi state: enough Germans supported this to enable it to happen; but those who knew of it and opposed it were too terrified to stand up against it for fear of what might happen to them or their families if they complained.

5. Why was Germany at War from 1939 to 1945?

Hitler wanted to destroy the Versailles Settlement, which he felt had emasculated Germany, and re-establish Germany as a great power in Europe, which he believed was her natural status. He also wanted to enlarge the German Reich to the east to give an expanding German population the living space that he felt it needed. Foreign policy, however, can never be conducted in a vacuum, and it was as much the attitudes of the other great European powers – France, Britain and Italy – and their policies of appeasement, as Hitler's aggressive foreign policy, that gave Germany control over Austria and Czechoslovakia and postponed war until 1939, when a miscalculation by Hitler forced him into a war that he did not want, with the Western powers rather than the Soviet Union.

To secure his western and southern flanks, and vital supplies of iron ore and oil, before turning east, Hitler had to be master of Europe. The stubborn refusal of Britain to submit dragged the war into 1941, when Hitler's patience ran out and he attacked the Soviet Union. Like Napoleon before him, he found Russia impossible to conquer, but his determination to succeed blinded him to the possibility of defeat, even to the extent of declaring war on the USA at the end of 1941. The shifting of the German economy on to a war footing, the earlier inability of the Allies to develop weapons capable of dramatically shortening the length of the war, the tight control of the German people by Nazi apparatus such as the SS, and the resilience of these people in the face of terrible hardships and privations extended the war for another three and a half years. Only when the country was close to becoming a wasteland did the German people cease to resist, and the Nazi Party follow Hitler to oblivion.

Hitler and Nazism

'Obviously, Nazism was a complex phenomenon to which many factors – social, economic, historical, psychological – contributed. But whatever the explanation of this episode in European history – and it can be no simple one – that does not answer the question with which this book has been concerned, what was the part played by Hitler. It may be true that a mass movement, strongly nationalist, anti-Semitic, and radical, would have sprung up in Germany without Hitler. But so far as what actually happened is concerned – not what might have happened – the evidence seems to me to leave no doubt that no other man played a role in the Nazi revolution or in the history of the Third Reich remotely comparable with that of Adolf Hitler.

The conception of the Nazi Party, the propaganda with which it must appeal to the German people, and the tactics by which it would come to power – these were unquestionably Hitler's. After 1934 there were no rivals left and by 1938 he had removed the last checks on his freedom of action. Thereafter he exercised an arbitrary rule in Germany to a degree rarely, if ever, equalled in a modern industrialised state.

… National Socialism produced nothing … The sole theme of the Nazi revolution was domination, dressed up as the doctrine of race …'

Alan Bullock, Hitler, 1962

As an exercise to allow you to participate in synthesising, extract the key points from the five different subheadings within this chapter. Note similarities and differences and, using the key skill of evaluation and your own knowledge, try and produce your own synthesis.

A-level questions rarely ask you to regurgitate all of your knowledge on a topic. Instead, they will ask you questions on certain aspects of a topic, and in your answer will be looking just as much at the skills you display in answering as at the knowledge that you have.

The six questions outlined in this section have been chosen to illustrate this, and have been adapted from A-level questions produced by the examination boards.

Question 1 asks you to look at Weimar Germany, but only to 1929, so it would not expect you to discuss the Great Depression.

It asks you to consider how stable and prosperous the Republic was by that date, and so clearly expects you to write about the period of the Republic from 1924 onwards, when it seemed to have recovered from the crises of the early 1920s.

However, in asking you about the accuracy of the statement, that Weimar was stable and prosperous, the question is asking you to make an assessment as to whether this was actually the case.

To do this, you must consider both the reality behind the apparent prosperity and stability, and the recent history of the Republic. Here you will find clues that the underlying nature of the economic and political structure of the regime was far from stable, and that Weimar was living an illusion in 1929. It would only require a minor upheaval (and the Depression was a major one) for the whole structure of the Republic to come crashing down.

Questions and Answers

1. How Accurate is it to Say that by 1929 Weimar Germany was a Stable and Prosperous State?

What you need to know about
The governments of the Republic, including the political parties, elections and the Weimar constitution; economic factors such as reparations, the hyperinflation and the recovery based on American loans; and social factors such as the relationship between the people and the politicians.

What you need to write about
The political situation in the Weimar Republic by 1929; the economic development of the country since 1918; and to what extent the stability and prosperity then apparent was real or illusory.

A suggested answer plan
1   Introduction. A summary of Germany in 1929: a rebuilt and reorganised industry, higher wages and consumer spending; economic growth for four years; political stability; a lively artistic and cultural life; Germany an equal European partner with France, Britain and Italy. All is apparently well.
2. The reality behind the economic prosperity. An economy dependent on American loans; the financial merry-go-round of reparations repayments; high unemployment and strike action; prosperity not shared equally; little saving.
3. The reality behind the political stability. The fragmentation of parties; many governments of shifting coalitions; the refusal of extreme right or left to work with the centre; a nationalist, right-wing President; a middle class not reconciled to the Republic.
4. The short-term nature of the prosperity. What had happened less than ten years before: the growing national debt; the huge reparations payments; the French occupation of the Ruhr; the hyperinflation that had ruined many.
5. The inherent instability of Weimar: proportional representation, and emergency presidential powers; its inheritance of acceptance of the Treaty of Versailles and overthrow of the old order; armed uprisings and the hostility of right and left.
6. Conclusion. Many Germans were unenthusiastic about the Republic. If economic prosperity went, which could happen given any change in world economic conditions, political stability would follow, as right and left would gain from the collapse of the centre.

2. To what Extent and why did Germans Vote for Hitler and the Nazi Party up to 1933?

What you need to know about

Weimar election results to 1933; a breakdown of German voters; the extent of Nazi penetration of each electoral group; the reasons behind the shifting allegiances of German voters; which German voters did not vote for the Nazis, and why, to 1933.

What you need to write about

Nazi support in the early and middle 1920s; Nazi Party organisation; the sharp rise in the Nazi vote after 1929; Nazi targeting of specific groups of voters; Nazi propaganda; the anti-Nazi vote; Nazi electoral violence.

A suggested answer plan

1   Introduction. The Nazi Party as a political force: its origins in Bavaria, its programme, style, uniforms and so on; its *Führer* principle and limited early support; its position on the far right of German politics and its internal organisation.

2.   Its transformation from a marginalised party to a major political force. Its position in 1929: a strong organisation and clear identity. The effect of the Great Depression on Germany, and the dissatisfaction of voters with the established political parties.

3.   Nazi propaganda techniques for targeting voters. The sections of the electorate targeted, and why: for peasant farmers relief from poverty, for women a return to family values and so on. The attractions of the Nazis to these groups: somewhere for the dispossessed to turn.

4.   Those not attracted to the Nazis, and why. The importance of existing organisations, such as trades unions or the Catholic church. The lack of support among the urban working class or liberals. A swing of support to the extreme left here.

5.   The effectiveness of Nazi campaigning: the brilliance of Hitler as a speaker; the mass rallies, music and flags to raise voter awareness; the importance of street-fighting and the aura of discipline; the importance of secret funds. The elections of 1930 and 1932.

6.   Conclusion. Nazi support came from different sections of the German people and for many different reasons: many of their promises were contradictory but sounded appealing. However, the Nazis made few inroads into existing organised groups, and never attracted more than 38% of the votes in elections to 1933.

Question 2 is not a question about the origins of the Nazi Party, and you must resist the temptation to write down all you know about Hitler's early life, *Mein Kampf* and so on. This is a question specifically about who and why voted for Hitler in the free and fair elections that were held under the Weimar Republic, and you should concentrate on discussing this.

There is no harm, and much good, in briefly describing what the Nazi Party was, and where it stood in the political spectrum. This positions it as a party of protest and helps to explain why it stood out as an alternative when the effects of the Depression made clear the bankruptcy of existing political parties.

The main thrust of the answer must be about the different interest groups in Germany, however, and why they were, or were not, attracted to vote for the Nazis. These groups must be clearly defined, and reasons for their voting patterns explained. You should also make it clear that not everyone in these groups would have voted in the same way, though you should note the things that would have made it more likely for them to vote one way rather than another.

Describe the effectiveness of Nazi campaigning; trace the patterns of voting across the 1930 and 1932 elections; and then summarise the overall weight of the Nazi vote.

At first sight, *question 3* is about the politics of the Weimar Republic. It is asking you about the politicians who ran the state and to what extent they can be held responsible for its failure.

However, if you are asked a question about the failure of the Weimar Republic, you have to consider the many reasons why it collapsed. Discussing politics in this context is not enough: you must bring in economic and social factors as well.

Try to outline why the Republic failed. Think about the Great Depression and its effects: how would this have changed the attitude of the voters in Weimar Germany. What could the politicians have done to cope with the crisis? More importantly, what did they do and was this enough?

You need to try to explain why votes for extremist parties rose as votes for moderate parties fell. Why did the democratic politicians not take matters into their own hands, or were they prevented from doing this by the Weimar system, which gave the opportunity for a few men to manipulate power?

This is a question with no right answers. As long as you can marshal your facts and arguments, and make a logical case for what you write, you should gain good marks.

3. 'The Weimar Republic Failed because its Politicians Lost Faith in Themselves.' To what Extent is this a Fair Statement?

What you need to know about

The political parties of the Republic; the Great Depression; presidential government: Brüning, Papen and Schleicher; the elections of 1930 and 1932; the rise of the Nazis and the Communists; Hindenburg and the conservative elites.

What you need to write about

The German economic crisis from 1929 to 1933 and its effects; the political deadlock in the Republic, leading to government by presidential decree; the rise of political extremism and the last days of the Republic.

A suggested answer plan

1. Introduction. The failure of the Republic was due to a complex set of political, economic and social circumstances. Each of these played a part in its downfall. It is over-simplistic to attribute its fall to a 'lack of faith' in politicians.

2. The key fact in the collapse of the Weimar Republic was economic, not political. The Great Depression, by causing the withdrawal of American loans from Europe, shattered Germany's apparent prosperity and threw the country into economic turmoil.

3. The closure of industries and banks, a dramatic rise in unemployment, falling food prices for farmers and a drastic cut in trade saw one-third of Germans living on the dole, and a popular demand for the politicians to do something.

4. It was not faith that the politicians lacked, but knowledge of how to cope with this unprecedented calamity. Most did not understand economics; few seemed able to grasp that this national disaster was far more important than all their petty differences. Their inactivity, however, and their willingness to accept presidential government, caused the German voters to lose faith with them.

5. Support for the Nazis and the Communists grew as that for the democratic politicians fell. Parliamentary government broke down as the Weimar system made majority rule impossible. Effective power passed to the conservative elites around the President, as backstairs intrigue caused chancellors to come and go until the appointment of Hitler.

6. Conclusion. The Great Depression shattered Germany's economy and the fragile stability of its political system. Germany's politicians were overwhelmed by events, and failed to solve her problems. The Weimar Republic ceased to be an effective form of government.

4. In what Ways, and how Successfully, did Nazi Germany Attempt to Deal with its Internal Opposition between 1933 and 1945?

What you need to know about

The Nazi seizure of power; the 'Night of the Long Knives'; individual and organised opposition; the army and the church; propaganda and indoctrination; the SS and the security services; the attempts to kill Hitler.

What you need to write about

The destruction of organised opposition groupings; the establishment of a police state; widespread persecution and indoctrination; the survival of opposition groups.

A suggested answer plan

1. Introduction. The Nazi illusion: careful use of propaganda and imagery portrays the Nazi state as a disciplined, united whole where self is subordinated to the group, all Germans march behind their *Führer*, and there is no deviation in thought, word or deed.

2. The reality. On coming to power the Nazis seize state governments, ban trades unions and dissolve other political parties. Thousands of people are arrested and imprisoned in concentration camps. The leaders of the SA are murdered. Hitler's henchmen are put in charge of the economy, workers organisations, culture and youth.

3. Propaganda and indoctrination are used to 'persuade' people that all is well under Nazi rule. The police and security services are greatly expanded. The Nazi Party is integrated into many aspects of German life. The *Gestapo* spies on everyone.

4. The political opponents of the Nazis form underground opposition groups and individuals make isolated protests against the regime. Churchmen and young people make life difficult for the authorities; and the Nazis have to make occasional gestures to keep civilian morale up and the population on their side in the war.

5. Most opposition is, however, crushed, and the brutality of the regime is increased as the opposition grows. More and more crimes become punishable by death; and thousands are rounded up and executed after the attempt to kill Hitler fails.

6. Conclusion. The Nazis never completely destroyed their internal opposition: it lived on to emerge in 1945. However, through the imposition of a police state the Nazis were extremely effective in curbing dissent. Only external opposition destroyed Hitler. Their internal enemies failed to overthrow the Nazis.

Internal opposition to the Nazis was widespread: but, again, *question 4* is not a descriptive question about who this opposition was or how it was organised. The question asks how this opposition was dealt with by the state, and how successfully; so knowledge of the organisations and powers of the state are here just as important as an awareness of the opposition to Hitler.

It is important to distinguish between illusion and reality. Describe how the Nazi state liked to portray itself, and then discuss what went on to rid the state of the opposition that it claimed not to have. Remember the passive techniques for keeping a population quiet – an unfree press, a directly controlled radio and so on – as well as the active techniques of a police state, such as spies, informants and no recourse to the law.

What was the opposition, and what measures did the regime take against it? You should indicate the growing nature of resistance to the Nazi state, and the increasing brutality of the response, especially after the plot to kill Hitler.

Conclude by assessing how successful the Nazi regime was in dealing with its enemies. Were they effective in limiting the nature of the regime, or were the Nazis able to push through their changes with little noticeable opposition from their foes?

Question 5 asks you about Hitler's foreign policy in the years before the Second World War, and it is tempting to think that what you have to do to answer it is describe the sequence of events that led to the outbreak of that conflict.

This is not the case. The question is much more about whether Hitler was following a policy directed towards a general European war than it is about the sequence of events leading to 1939 itself.

What you must do here is to use your knowledge of European foreign policy between 1933 and 1939 as a framework on which to hang the questions of Hitler's aims and intentions.

What the question is asking you to do is to consider the debate between the 'Intentionalists' and the 'Structuralists'. It wants your assessment of whether Hitler was following a step-by-step approach towards war, or whether he was swept along by events.

It wants you to look at his actions over the Rhineland, Austria and Czechoslovakia and consider which way he was heading. It wants you to think about the actions of the other European powers, and consider whether their actions encouraged Hitler to alter his aims. It wants you to consider Hitler's views in *Mein Kampf* and his dreams of *Lebensraum*.

Try to work these assessments into your answer. If you come to a different answer to me, don't worry. As long as you can justify your conclusions, you will gain good marks.

5. Was General War the Intended Result of the Aims and Conduct of Hitler's Foreign Policy, from 1933 to 1939?

What you need to know about

Hitler's ideas from *Mein Kampf*; his early moves in power; the march into the Rhineland; the foreign policy objectives of Britain, France and Italy; Austria, Czechoslovakia and Poland; the debate between the 'Intentionalists' and the 'Structuralists'.

What you need to write about

General German, and specifically Nazi, foreign policy aims; the importance of the Versailles settlement; Hitler's increasingly expansionist foreign policy; the attitude of the other European powers to Hitler's moves; the outbreak of war – intention or mistake?

A suggested answer plan

1. Introduction. The debate between the historians. Did Hitler have a plan for world conquest, or was he swept along by events? The importance of the other players: foreign policy cannot take place in a vacuum – the reaction of other nations to what Hitler did was as important as his original actions.

2. The evidence. Hitler's aims as expressed in *Mein Kampf*, and other places. Was this a programme for action or a hoped-for dream? His early moves: breaking Versailles and marching into the Rhineland. Were these first steps to world power or re-establishing Germany in Europe?

3. The reaction of other countries. Why did Britain and France not defend Versailles more vigorously? Did their reluctance to act against Hitler encourage him to go further than he would have? What was the role of Italy? How important to Hitler were his foreign policy successes?

4. A Greater German Reich. By 1938 Hitler was confident enough to take over Austria and demand, and get, the Czech Sudetenland. Did appeasement encourage him? Could a more robust line by Britain and France have stopped him at Munich?

5. The break-up of Czechoslovakia, and Poland. Britain and France guaranteed Polish security, but there was nothing they could do to save the country. They then declared war on Germany, and not the other way round. Hitler was surprised. Is this significant?

6. Conclusion. What were Hitler's aims? A greater German *Reich* with *Lebensraum* in Poland and Russia? Certainly; but a general European war? Probably not. After re-establishing Germany as a great European power, Hitler's thrust was always to the east: the war he found himself with in 1939 was one that he did not want.

6. How Successfully did the Nazis Tackle the Problems of Germany's Economy between 1933 and 1945?

What you need to know about

The German economy in 1933; Nazi policies on trade, rearmament and unemployment, and for agriculture and business; the German economy during the war years; the use of slave labour and the SS industrial concerns.

What you need to write about

The collapse of the German economy in the Great Depression; its regeneration under the Nazis; the artificial nature of the new economy; and its destruction during the Second World War.

A suggested answer plan

1. Introduction. The German economy in 1933: mass unemployment; the closure of banks and factories; poverty for many people; and the part this played in the collapse of the Weimar Republic, and in bringing the Nazis to power.
2. How the Nazis claimed to have solved German unemployment: public works, boosting trade, autarky, rearmament, conscription. Describe the course of each of these and how they reduced the unemployment figures.
3. The artificial nature of the new employment. Were these real jobs, how were the figures massaged, could this vast public investment have continued, and what was the inevitable outcome of an economy gearing itself up for war?
4. Agriculture, business, the industrial workers: Nazi policy in these areas. How what they claimed to do was not always the same as what was delivered. The conflict between Schacht and Göring. Was the economy well managed anyway?
5. The war years. The *Blitzkrieg* economy of 1939–1941 contrasted with the total war economy from 1942. The policies of Todt and Speer; the use of women and forced labour in the factories; the obscenities of the SS industrial cartels.
6. Conclusion. Was the German economy successful under the Nazis? Did it produce the goods that the people, or the state, wanted? Was it efficient, or wasteful of resources? How did it compare in the war years to Britain and America? Could a more successful economy have prospered under Nazism anyway?

Question 6 is another where you need to assess rather than describe. You should also note that this question does not limit itself to Germany's peacetime economy, but asks you to consider the wartime economy too, up to 1945. This means that you will have to bring two areas of knowledge together, and fuse them to create one seamless answer.

Remember that the great Nazi claim was to have succeeded in getting Germany back to work. Analyse this claim to see if it stands up. What was the state of the German economy in 1933, and what did the Nazis do to change it? Describe their policies and assess how they got unemployment down; but don't be afraid to query these policies if you feel that they failed to cure 'real' unemployment, or only worked because of massive state investment.

The problems of Germany's economy were also more than unemployment. Agriculture and trade were just as important, as was macro-economic policy. Was this handled well? Carry on looking at the German economy into the war years. When did it change from a peacetime to a wartime one; what were the effects of this; how did the SS and the *Gauleiter* local officials compete for scarce resources, and was this an efficient use of such resources?

Conclude by assessing the Nazis' handling of the German economy over 12 years. Was it a total success, a partial one, or was it bound to deliver in the way that it did because of the political and social restraints placed upon it?

Adolf Hitler

It is very easy to see Adolf Hitler as a demon. Popular mythology has it that he was power-crazed, a tyrant who wanted to rule all Europe and who deliberately took Germany into a world-wide war in order to destroy Britain and the other democracies. He has often been portrayed as a wild-eyed madman, chewing the carpet in his rages.

Hitler may have been power-hungry, and aspects of his regime were certainly demonic; but a serious study of Hitler should depict him as the serious political leader that he was, as a man who, having come through the trials of the Great War, was able to found, mould and control a party which, however abhorrent, was a disciplined force with a clear and distinctive political message.

Moreover, Hitler took the opportunities given to him. He used the upset of the Great Depression to make his party a genuine political force; he seized his chance as Chancellor to force through the revolution that gave him absolute power; he did not hesitate to crush Röhm and the SA; and he exploited the weakness of Britain and France in the 1930s to prosecute an aggressive foreign policy.

That he used his political genius for evil rather than good is a tragedy that the whole world came to regret. You should not let your feelings about his regime obscure the fact of his achievements: but neither should the fact that he was a man – and not a devil – hide the real nature of the evil that he and his regime perpetrated.

Final Review

This book has been about the history of Germany between 1918 and 1945. It is a popular fallacy that these are the years of the Nazis: in fact, the Third Reich covered only 12 of those years. The remainder of that time (and the majority of it) was the era of the Weimar Republic, a liberal and democratic system of government that was in stark contrast to the totalitarian dictatorship that was to come.

However, if history is about anything it is about people, and the one man who dominated these years must be Adolf Hitler. True, he was unknown outside Germany for a decade, and he was a very minor player on the political stage inside the country for that time; but from the onset of the Great Depression he, and the political party that he founded, had a profound influence first on Germany, then on Europe, and finally on the world. For good or ill (and it was mostly ill), Adolf Hitler was one of the key shapers of the 20th century.

The Weimar Republic is important in this story, because it sets the Third Reich in context. Anything, from a Communist revolution to an army takeover, could have come out of Germany's defeat in 1918. That a liberal and democratic government with a fair measure of popular support should have emerged seemed both remarkable at the time and a great hope for the future. It appeared that a new member was joining the 'club' of the Western parliamentary democracies, in time for the new era of world peace that the League of Nations seemed to presage. Even the initial problems of armed uprisings, hyperinflation and near economic collapse were seen as just the birth-pangs of a new order. When the Republic did collapse, ten years later, in a welter of economic crisis, political inertia and popular discontent, the shock was all the greater, especially as it was replaced by a repressive regime, apparently brought to power by the will of the people.

As you now realise, there was a lot more to it than that. Hitler and the Nazi Party had a long apprenticeship, learning both political in-fighting and street-fighting in the months and years when it appeared that the organisation was going nowhere fast, and heading for oblivion. It was the Depression that gave Hitler his chance, enabling him and his party to put into effect all of the techniques that they had learned in their years in the wilderness, and sweep up the protest votes of people who felt themselves let down by the established political organisations. Yet this would not have been enough to allow them to come to power if it had not been for the inability of the established political parties in Germany to work together, or for the intrigues of the conservative elites who gave Hitler power in the belief that they could tame him.

The Nazi state that came into existence proved to be unlike anything seen in European history before. It shared similarities with both fascism and communism, but proved to be much more efficient and racist than the first, while being far more militaristic, but chaotic, than the second. It sprang from the ideas of one man, translated into the ideology of a political party, and was in many ways revolutionary in outlook, while at the same time harking back to a mythical age of Aryan purity and Germanic greatness that placed it firmly in the past.

The Nazis attempted a 'social revolution' in Germany, trying to change the very way in which people thought and acted, but ultimately failed in this, as they were unable to upset the deeply entrenched culture and traditions of a modern European nation. However, by playing on some of the darker fears of the people, and by being determined enough to press through with their policies, they were able to scapegoat an entire section of the German nation, with very little resistance from the rest of it, and destroy them. The genocide, carried out against the European Jewish community, and against gypsies, homosexuals, and the physically and mentally handicapped, was a crime without parallel in history.

Hitler's policies, whether he meant them to or not, also unleashed the most devastating of all modern wars. The Second World War, either directly or indirectly, killed over 50 million people, shattered an entire continent, ushered in the age of the Cold War and had precisely the opposite effect on Germany that Hitler had intended. Hitler had expected his Third Reich to last for a thousand years, and that its inclusion of all European Germans in a united country that would dominate central and eastern Europe would be his most enduring legacy.

Yet the legacy that Hitler left behind was of a divided Germany and Europe, a Europe no longer central to world affairs but a battleground between the two new great powers of the USA and the USSR. Because of the way the war turned, 1945 saw Russian troops in control of much of eastern Europe while American forces dominated the west. The wartime Allies, with their competing ideologies, soon fell out, and the division of Germany into control zones soon became permanent. A western German state was divided from an eastern one by guards, minefields and barbed wire, as capitalism and communism strove for supremacy, and the German people found themselves pawns in a wider and more deadly game. Only the collapse of communism in eastern Europe, and the subsequent fall of the USSR itself saw Germany reunite and emerge once more as a European power, able to influence the destiny of a converging continent. It owed none of this to Hitler and the Nazis: they were now confined to the pages of History.

The Nazi Party

The Nazi Party was not the all-embracing force that the Communist Party was in the USSR. There was no strict hierarchy, no formal chains of command, nothing to hold the party together, under the various organisational bosses, other than Hitler.

The party *Gaue*, the Teachers' League, the Hitler Youth, the SA and SS, the Reich Chamber of Culture – none of these had anything in common save for the fact that one had to be a Nazi Party member to rise up the ladder in any of them. Even the membership was broken and fractured. What did a teacher have in common with a painter, or a bureaucrat, or a brawling street-thug?

The Nazi Party membership was diverse: the millions who joined and stayed did so for a whole variety of reasons, ranging from the idealistic to the opportunistic. It is probably incorrect, therefore, to talk of the Nazi Party as if it were a coherent whole. It was much more a series of groupings, each group having its own interests to defend and promote.

The one thing that held these disparate groups together was loyalty to the *Führer*. This fact was central to the success of the Nazi Party in Germany. Without this loyalty the party might have splintered under the centrifugal forces that were pulling it apart.

The German people

The main beneficiaries, and victims, of Hitler's rule were the German people. Many rose to undreamt-of heights of power and influence; many others suffered as few had suffered before. At the end, in 1945, few escaped the consequences of the Third Reich.

As discussed elsewhere, it is incorrect, however, to talk of the German people as if this was one single organism. The German people were over 50 million individuals, each of whom had his or her own identity, thoughts and feelings.

It is possible to break these people up into groups – the peasantry, the middle class, industrial workers, and so on – and it is possible to make generalised statements about each group. However, when making such statements it always has to be borne in mind that such statements are generalised, and do not necessarily apply to everyone within that group.

That seems a very obvious thing to say, but it is surprising how often one reads that, for example, the German working class were solidly anti-Nazi, when it is quite clear that many of them must have been distinctly pro-Nazi, in order to make up the 2 million men in the SA.

Take care when writing about people in Germany in the Nazi era: only say what you are sure that you mean.

Knowledge of the Nazi period should no longer be confined to the 'pages' of History, however. As I have argued elsewhere, historical information now comes in many forms, and you will not have the breadth of knowledge to study this topic if you do not take account of this. In the past few years the world has gone through an information revolution, and one way of viewing history – on the television screen, in pictures, or on the page – is now just as valid as another.

The other key element to studying History remains, as it always has done, the depth of the information available, although even here technology has improved the availability of the information. Reading other people's work remains, at A-level, the best introduction to a subject; but if you want to acquire the level of knowledge necessary, you must look at primary sources to deepen your understanding of the topic.

The 'great and the good' have always published diaries, letters and autobiographies, explaining the decisions they took at key times, excusing their mistakes and taking credit for their good deeds. Sometimes, too, the foot-soldiers of history have left accounts of what it was like to live at certain times and take part in the events that others initiated or controlled. All too often, however, this detail is lost, as the need to put it down on paper has come between the person and what he or she wants to say.

The Hitler era is one of the first to which this no longer applies. As well as the wealth of official documentation, film, audio and television have recorded hundreds, if not thousands, of interviews with the participants of this history, allowing the researcher unprecedented access to the lives and minds of ordinary people. In addition to this, quantitative techniques brought to the analysis of some areas of History – for example, voting patterns from published results in towns and villages – allow the historian to assess with much greater accuracy how specific groups of people within an area felt and thought, and to replace the vague generalisation with a much more precise targeting.

Your knowledge at A-level should aim to be as precise. It is no longer possible to 'get away with' a generalised knowledge of the Third Reich or Weimar Germany gleaned from books intended for the general reader. By all means make these your starting point, but from then on think about the core issues that you have to address, consider the different questions that you could raise, assess the notes that you need to make, and then find the information that you need, looking always for the detail that is going to show the examiner that you have a thorough grasp of your subject.

Lastly, remember that all through this book you have been practising skills, which are just as central to A-level History as the knowledge and understanding that you have gained and the detailed information that you have found. These skills should have enabled you to order events, to identify and evaluate sources of evidence, and to explain critically different interpretations of events.

You should now be able to investigate an event, or series of events. You should have in your mind questions to ask of what happened and you should be able to look for information that you feel will give you answers. You should know where to look, and what to ask for if you cannot find what you want. You should be prepared to use all types of information, and read around a subject – picking out the relevant information that you need.

You should be able to analyse what you have discovered. This means not just accepting what has been said, but comparing information between sources, discussing what you have found with teachers or other students, and ultimately using your own judgement to decide whether or not something is reasonable.

You should be able to explain events and interpret them. This means not simply knowing what happened, but why and how it happened. It also means being able to compare two different versions of the same event and, considering the available evidence, being able to decide which of the versions is the more accurate and likely.

If you come across various factors in your research that seem to answer a question, you should be able to assess them. Each will be of some importance or significance: but you should be able to weight them, to say which are more important than others, and why. Most things have more than one explanation: you should be able to sort the central from the incidental.

Above all, you should be able to empathise with the period. This is one of the hardest skills to acquire because it is so subjective, but what it really means is being able to understand not just the events of a historical period, but also the attitudes that lay behind them. In different times and in different places, people have behaved in ways that seem incomprehensible to us – but to them, living in a different culture with different values and different beliefs, it all seemed perfectly natural. This is not to excuse barbarism, greed or ignorance, but to try to understand the forces that drove people to do the things that they did, and why they might not have felt guilty about them. We might never vote for fascism or national socialism but, as someone once wrote, 'The past is a foreign country: they do things differently there'.

History and the Nazis

The Nazi era continues to fascinate people: but for how much longer?

Already, those who had direct experience of the Nazis are in their sixties or over, and are grandparents. In one more generation there will be few alive who have seen a swastika fly in anger. When they are gone, who will remember?

The course of history continues. The Cold War succeeded the Nazi era, and yet too that now is history as we enter the post Cold War world, with communism looking likely to follow fascism to the scrap heap. Should we continue to remember something that has no direct relevance to us any more?

I would argue 'Yes'. Hitler may have gone the way of Napoleon or Charlemagne, but the things that he represented – intolerance, hate and ignorance – survive. The flowering of small neo-Nazi groups in Europe, the genocide in Cambodia and Rwanda, and the terrorist atrocities of the Middle East show that the spirit of Hitler is all too alive.

If we forget what happened in Europe in the 20th century, we run the risk of it happening again, somewhere else in the world, in the 21st.

Those who do not remember the past are condemned to repeat it

Index